Prayer
Notes
to a
Friend

Ed Hays' books always enrich and nourish me, and he does it again, in his newest book, Prayer Notes to a Friend. *As you turn pages, it's like having a comforting spiritual director at your elbow. Reading Fr. Ed's prayer notes is a perfect way to recollect your thoughts so you can live prayerfully each day. I highly recommend it.*

—**Barbara Bartocci**, author, *Nobody's Child Anymore* and *From Hurting to Happy: Transforming Your Life After Loss*

In this, his latest literary sharing, Edward Hays allows his readers the privilege of peering over his shoulder as he corresponds with friends and soul companions on a variety of personal and provocative issues. Offering sound spiritual advice and original insights into the Mystery Who is God, Hays leads those who would accompany him on a voyage of faith. Exploring uncharted realms and making stopovers for "Emmaus meals," Hays engages his readers in table conversation over such interesting topics as the Cactus Prayer, Shadow Dancing, the Sacrifice of the Tongue, P-Mail, the Bartender's Prayer, and the Blessed Bolsheviks. Like a trusty and seasoned guide, Hays points the path and suggests an itinerary but does not prod, and those who accept him as their Anam Cara (Irish for "Soul Friend") will find their expedition marked by intriguing and even tantalizing spiritual discoveries. As per his recommendation, voyagers should allot ample time for pondering Hays' brief prayer notes so as to allow them to permeate their souls and prompt their practical and personal application. Given the fact of our chronically time-impoverished lifestyles, some may find Hays' invitation to ponder a prodigal waste of time. In response, Hays insists that time is necessary for discovering what God has chosen to "write between the lines." Those who have traveled with Hays before know that their time will be well spent and that theirs will be an enlightening and exciting trip. Novice pilgrims will delight in making that discovery for themselves.

—**Patricia Datchuck Sánchez**, author, educator

Prayer Notes

to a Friend

Edward Hays

FOREST OF PEACE
Publishing

Suppliers for the Spiritual Pilgrim
Leavenworth, KS

Other Books by the Author:
(available through Forest of Peace Publishing or your favorite bookstore)

Prayers and Rituals

Psalms for Zero Gravity
Prayers for a Planetary Pilgrim
Prayers for the Domestic Church
Prayers for the Servants of God

Parables and Stories

Little Orphan Angela
The Gospel of Gabriel
The Quest for the Flaming Pearl
St. George and the Dragon
The Magic Lantern
The Ethiopian Tattoo Shop
Twelve and One-Half Keys
Sundancer
The Christmas Eve Storyteller

Contemporary Spirituality

The Great Escape Manual
The Ladder
The Old Hermit's Almanac
The Lenten Labyrinth
A Lenten Hobo Honeymoon
Holy Fools & Mad Hatters
A Pilgrim's Almanac
Pray All Ways
Secular Sanctity
In Pursuit of the Great White Rabbit
The Ascent of the Mountain of God
Feathers on the Wind

Prayer Notes to a Friend

copyright © 2002, by Edward M. Hays

Library of Congress Cataloging-in-Publication Data

Hays, Edward M.
    Prayer notes to a friend / Edward Hays.
      p. cm.
    ISBN 0-939516-66-7. — ISBN 0-939516-67-5 (pbk.)
    1. Prayer—Christianity. I. Title.
  BV210.3 .H39 2002
  248.3'2—dc21   2002007363

published by
Forest of Peace Publishing, Inc.
PO Box 269
Leavenworth, KS 66048-0269   USA
1-800-659-3227
www.forestofpeace.com

printed by
Hall Commercial Printing
Topeka, KS 66608-0007

Calligraphy art and cover design by Edward Hays

1st printing: September 2002

Dedicated to

My friends and soul companions
to whom these notes were written
whose names are listed below
in invisible ink

Prayer Note Themes

Author's Preface

Originally the Prayer Notes in this book began with an idea of sporadically sending short notes about prayer to a few close friends with whom I share conversations about the spiritual life. Early in the pregnancy of this inspiration I began jotting down ideas I thought would be helpful for the friends receiving these Prayer Notes.

As the number of Prayer Notes began to grow, so did my concern about the amount of time and work involved in addressing and mailing them. Logically, the easiest way would be to send them by the relatively effortless vehicle of e-mail, and I confess I entertained that temptation. In the past I staunchly resisted any use of e-mail, realizing it could easily escalate into a-mail — an avalanche of correspondence. Perhaps my infatuation with remaining an electronically celibate hermit provided the grace to resist that temptation. Then, in the midst of deliberating about the project I had a surprise visitor. It was an inspiration that said, "Edward, your notes could become the genesis of a manuscript for a small book intended for both known and unknown friends." And thus was birthed the book you are presently holding in your hands.

How to Use This Notebook

My hope is that you will use this book as I originally desired that my friends would, as brief reflections that could be pondered and then practiced. Pondering takes time. Contemporary life, being chronically time-impoverished, requires making quick decisions. So you may be challenged to "sit with" a Prayer Note long enough for it to be seeded in your busy life. Also, you'll be tempted whenever a particular Note appears to lack any personal application to turn the page quickly. I encourage you to resist that temptation. Read the entry again, and perhaps wait a day and then read it a third time.

Why this prodigal waste of time? Because often the most beneficial and far-reaching effects begin with an indirect application. As the Portuguese say, "God writes straight with crooked lines." Personally, I've discovered that God consistently writes between the lines.

My Dear Friend,

As I begin to write this note to you, my salutation makes me conscious of the difference between conversation and correspondence. Personally, I would find it awkward to address you in public as "Dear Friend," and yet the proper style for a formal letter is to begin with "Dear Sir" or "Dear Madam," even to someone I don't know. When I add the pronoun "My" to that greeting, it becomes even more intimate.

True friendship is dear. So precious is a true friend, one who is willing to share his or her life and soul experiences with you. In our society there are two things never shared except with a truly intimate friend, or perhaps a confessor — one's sexual and soul encounters! And of these two, our soul or spiritual experiences — like prayer and our encounters with God — are less likely to be exposed to another, even to our spouses. Whatever the reason, be it the fear that our soul life is too shabby to be shared or that our prayers are inadequate, the fact is that people avoid talking about their inner lives. The general rule seems to be: politics and even religion are acceptable, but not the soul. Yet by mutual agreement, you and I do talk about the adventures of our souls, our successes and failures at prayer, and we exchange questions about the Spirit life.

I reject the title of Spiritual Director, feeling myself to be a perpetual student of the Spirit life. Since I have not yet mastered the art of the soul, I also disclaim the role of a Spiritual Master, with you as a student. We are both students. We are friends and companions sharing the same quest. So, then, who or what am I? I prefer to consider myself your soul friend, your Anam Cara, as the Irish say.

Also, you and I do not have spiritual conferences! We simply have visits about prayer and God, usually over a meal and often afterwards expanded into a leisurely walk where we continue our conversation. I enjoy calling our visits, our luncheon conversations, "Emmaus Meals." You know well the story in Luke's Gospel about the two disciples on the road to Emmaus who share deeply their sorrow and spiritual feelings after the crucifixion. As they break bread in their roadside meal in a secular setting, they experience the presence of Christ, which is what happens for me in our meals.

As we explore new areas of prayer and the spiritual life, may these Prayer Notes I write to you be expansions of our Emmaus luncheon visits and new occasions to encounter resurrection life.

My Dear Friend,

In the midst of your time-crunched way of life, it's not surprising that you would wrestle with the notion of "praying always." Yet when you understand that air is to the body what prayer is to the soul, you realize why the Master told us to "pray unceasingly." To live more than a couple of minutes without air is impossible, yet to be constantly praying seems equally impossible. After all, humans breathe over 23,000 times each day. Imagine attempting to pray that many times each day!

Prayer is communion and contact with the Source of Life. You might even call prayer your soul's umbilical cord contact with its Life Source. Since by its very nature your soul is constantly in communion with God, it is perpetually praying. In that light, you might consider making the energizing enterprise of becoming more and more conscious of your soul as the nucleus of your spiritual activity. As awareness of your soul grows, your life is enlivened by the energy of the perpetual adoration of your soul and spirit.

Being absent-minded is not having misplaced your mind but, rather, is simply being forgetful. Similarly, being absent-souled is being forgetful, forgetful of your divine contact. The act of prayer reconnects and reminds you of that imperceptible aspect of yourself called your soul.

The Infinitely Inventive Soul Maker created in you an

absolutely unique and unparalleled soul. God loves originals. Just as you have unmatchable fingerprints, so your soul print is equally distinctive. Remember that today, and everything and everyone you touch will be marked with your soul print.

I encourage you as often as possible today to strive in everything you do with all your heart and soul so you can be ceaselessly and consciously praying.

My Dear Friend,

The Age of Exploration has not ended, nor has your personal primal urge to explore the unknown. This primordial craving to go beyond the familiar still slumbers in your soul. Even if you are eager to go off on an expedition of discovery, what's left to be discovered? What mountains are left unclimbed, what jungles, rivers or deserts unmapped?

The first half of life is consumed with exploring and developing our bodies, educating our minds and cultivating our talents. Midlife is an ideal time to venture into the unknown, the territory of your soul. Over the past millennia an understanding of the soul has slowly developed. The Greeks gave us the idea of it being the spiritual principle of life and a reality that is distinct from the body. Christian scriptures recognized it as a living consciousness, as one's very self, having an immortal character. Our faith affirms that each human has only one soul, directly created by God simultaneously with the body. While giving intellectual and religious assent to these concepts, how microscopic is our everyday consciousness of this mysterious inner reality?

Prayer is your vessel for the most adventuresome of all discovery expeditions — the exploration of your soul. The scope of this great adventure can be heightened by contemplating the notion that we are souls with bodies rather than bodies with souls. From this perspective, the body exists within the soul, your soul having a radius larger than your body.

Reflect on these lines from Shakespeare's play *Julius Caesar* if you are debating whether or not to depart on such a soul expedition:

> There is a tide in the affairs of men
> Which taken at the flood leaves on to fortune,
> Omitted and they spend
> The rest of their lives in the shallows.

My Dear Friend,

By means of these notes you and I have set sail on a soul quest. It truly is a mutual voyage, which is to say that I'm not just accompanying you on the quest. In the process we are both discovering new aspects of prayer, and I find myself energized by the enterprise.

When you think about it, the souls of discoverers like Christopher Columbus and Ferdinand Magellan must have been invested with a special zest for exploring. Like their predecessors down through primitive times, they set forth without maps or guides.

You are more fortunate than they, for you do have a map for your spirit-voyage, the same kind of chart you use countless times a day to find anything — a memory map. Souls have memories; in fact, etched in your soul is a remembrance of the moment it was given to you. This recollection includes the image of your Soul Maker, who with great affection created a soul specifically for you. Usually our prebirth memories remain dormant and unused until seconds before our last breath, but they can be activated at any point in our voyage of exploration. Indeed, memory maps hold magnetic power; allow the map of your soul to magnetically draw you both consciously and unconsciously toward the unexplored — the Great Divine Unknowable. Author John O'Donohue says, "A world lives within you," and your destination is that unexplored world of your soul. As I said in my last note, it is a spiritual journey that transforms as well as transports you.

While your soul's memory is subterranean, it daily speaks to you! It expresses itself in your every desire for more: more affection, more security, more comfort, more of everything. Your unquenchable hunger for something new or different is only the throbbing of your soul-map. Instead of suppressing these desires or responding to them, consider each of them as a homing signal implanted in the memory of your soul. Then rejoice, for explorer souls that are awake are inordinately greedy, unscrupulously eager to find more of God in everything.

The next time you experience the craving to purchase something new, pause and ask yourself if that object is what your soul really desires. You may find that your desire isn't for anything new, but rather is a nostalgic aching for something old. More than old, it is so ancient as to be eternal.

P.S. One of the rules of the soul is: "Be greedy — never be content, always want more and more of the Invisible."

My Dear Friend,

Like many others on the path of prayer, you and I have struggled with the practice of self-denial. Indeed, classic spirituality is one of subtraction. It proclaims that the surest way to reach God is by subtracting, an emptying out of self in order to be filled with the Divine Mystery. This classical principle is found in all the world's great religions, where those who are the emptiest are the holiest. Subtraction Spirituality is expressed in Catholic Christianity by the three religious vows of poverty, chastity and obedience. For a millennium and a half these vows of renouncing possession of property, enjoyment of sexual love, and self-direction have provided a fertile path to holiness for serious seekers of God.

Vows in marriage and religious life focus the energy of your soul. Yet at this point in your spiritual growth, instead of the Vow of Poverty I propose the Vow of Plenty. As a way to God this new promise of plenty is diametrically opposed to the venerable spiritual subtraction because it dedicates you to zealously pursuing an extravagantly bountiful life. Even a casual glance at creation reveals how this is God's Way, because God is profusely lavish to an excess. This Vow of Plenty is an expression of a Superlative Spirituality, in which you daily strive to a love of life, God, self, friend, family and neighbor in an unsurpassingly generous way.

Those who take the Vow of Plenty are recognized

because they never get enough of God. They constantly want more and more of the Mystery. They never get enough of love, life, beauty, prayer and intimacy. While the majority only nibbles around on the edges of creation, these vowed seekers are gluttons at the feast of genesis. They are not benefactors who limit their gifts to God to a meager 10%; rather, they are extravagantly generous, overindulgent lovers, excessively patient, intemperately forgiving.

My Dear Friend,

I realize these reflections on the nature of your soul can seem difficult since we are not dealing with a tangible reality. However, while intangible, your soul is not like static air sealed in an airtight bottle of flesh, motionless, passionless and unfeeling. The Psalms of David provide rich models for your prayer, for they speak of the soul as hungering, thirsting and being tormented by its own urges and longings. They are soul-conscious prayers: "To you, O God, I lift up my soul...," "My soul clings to you...," "The Law of God refreshes my soul...."

In her beautiful canticle Mary the Mother of Christ sang joyfully of how her soul magnified — enlarged — the Lord, and how her soul rejoiced in God her liberator. In his Olive Garden agony Jesus experienced the depths of his soul's sorrow and dark distress, the acidity of its bitterness. For him, as for all Israelites, humans were seen as "ensouled" — their body and soul wedded with life — and so he experienced his soul as having great appetites and emotions.

If to Jesus' understanding of his soul you add your Christian belief that God creates a unique soul for each person, then prepare to be astonished. That would imply the experiences of your soul are divinely different from those of any other soul ever created.

In your quest to probe your infinite inner world, realize

how many are the senses of your soul. The voice of your soul, for example, is expressed in silent thoughts. When some fleeting thought of a friend, a family member or a sick acquaintance enters your mind, realize that such thoughts are soul prayers. By your very thinking of them you are praying for them. Your soul also has ears for messages of inspiration, and cultivated souls can clearly hear the silent cries of those who are suffering. In addition, your soul sees. In both beauty and ugliness, it perceives the Divine hidden beneath a thin veneer of flesh, fin or feather. This soul vision recognizes the to-be-loved neighbor in the friend and stranger, and has a white-cane-tapping sight of the sacred that is subtly hidden in the mundane. Furthermore, your soul has the sense of touch. Your fingertips are soul extensions when you handle the common objects of daily life with a reverence usually reserved for the vessels of the altar.

A final recollection: Mindful of how often others are in your thoughts, rejoice that you are ceaselessly praying soul prayers.

My Dear Friend,

In these Notes to you about acquiring a deeper appreciation for your soul and how it completely penetrates every atom of your body, I've realized that I have a problem. My problem is contained in a two-letter word in that opening sentence. The body isn't just a fleshly container for your soul. This attitude is a Greek concept that is responsible for much of Christianity's negative attitude toward our bodies. Your soul is intimately one with the flesh, bone and blood of your body, which it energizes, vitalizes and infuses. This total permutation of a human soul is with a human body, complete with its sexual identity. Here lies my problem of pronouns: Instead of referring to your soul as "it," should I not be using a personal pronoun?

It would be unthinkable to refer to God as the "Almighty It" since we have a personal relationship with God, the Divine Spirit. Shouldn't the same be the case with your spirit and your soul? So, my friend, whenever speaking to or about your soul, I encourage you to use the proper personal pronoun befitting your gender.

Perhaps in the coming years of this twenty-first century, already marked by an array of amazing technological inventions, some genius will create a microchip sexual-sensor-device that publishers and printers will implant in their books. The sensor will be able to detect the gender or sexual orientation of the reader and automatically change all the pronouns into the appropriate ones for that reader and for God. While awaiting that scientific breakthrough, as an author I'm left with only two options; the use of "he/she" when referring to your soul, or to continue using "it." I have chosen the latter. I do so urging you as strongly as possible to substitute for yourself the correct pronoun each time "it" appears.

My Dear Friend,

Today in my reading I came across a beautiful quotation by Walt Whitman that touched upon our visit of the other day, during which you spoke of your difficulty in thinking of your body and soul as sharing a mutual experience. We discussed how the stlye of religious education in days past continues to haunt us with a sort of split spiritual personality of the body versus the soul. So I offer you these lines from Whitman's poem "I Sing the Body Electric" for your reflection:

> O my body! I dare not desert the likes of you in other men
> And women, nor the likes of the parts of you.
> I believe the likes of you are to stand or fall with
> The likes of the soul, (and that they are the soul...)

Whitman's poetic identification of the beauties of the body with those of the soul should inspire you to abstain from "separating what God has joined together," to quote from the marriage rite. Whitman's notion that the likes of the body stand or fall with those of the soul should alert you to how critical is your prayerful formation of a positive, soul-infused relationship with your body. His inclusion of the entire body with the words "...nor the likes of the parts of you" challenges your ingrained and usually unconscious religious condemnation of certain parts of the body as being unclean and sinfully inclined.

Anything ingrained is usually indelibly stained and thus is extremely difficult to remove. So whenever some shameful body thought spontaneously arises, cleanse yourself by praying for the gift of God-sight. Pray for the grace to look upon your body with God's eyes, which see the body as soul-saturated and awesomely beautiful. You might easily be inclined to think this advice doesn't apply to you since you have outgrown that old negative religious attitude about the human body. Be vigilant, however, for destructive and self-injurious attitudes about your body are both deeply ingrained and constantly being reinforced by both society and religion. Soul-body self-cleansing may have to be one of life's ongoing prayers.

Whenever you become conscious of your body while dressing or bathing, pray a wordless prayer that you will never desert your body, nor any parts of it, for some artificial spiritual state of holiness.

My Dear Friend,

In the spiritual catalog of images, your soul is allocated the images of breath, spirit and air. Their primary biblical source is the Genesis story of God bringing Adam to life by breathing into his nostrils. Since it isn't easy to give an image to the invisible, I offer you the following new account of the Genesis story.

In the beginning, after already creating abundantly different kinds of birds, fish and animals, the Creator was inspired to make something new. God the Potter knelt down by the river in Eden and scooped up handfuls of wet clay. "Let us make ourselves a human, whom we'll call Adam," said the Divine Potter, creatively shaping a hunk of damp clay into the beautiful body of the first human. Adam, however, lay lifeless on the earth from which he had been formed with his eyelids closed. God was surprised, not having previously encountered a lifeless creation in the other days of creation.

But God had a visitation, an inspiration. Taking up a bucket, God went down to the riverbank and filled it with water. Returning to the lifeless creature Adam, God poured the entire bucket of water into his nostrils and mouth and waited. The beautiful earthen body didn't stir a twitch. Not defeated, the Creator returned again to the river, filling the bucket full a second time and emptying it into Adam. Nothing happened. Bucket after bucket, a third, fourth and fifth time, God poured water into Adam's nostrils and mouth. After emptying the fifth bucket, Adam opened one eye and then the other. Overjoyed, God raced to the river and back again, quickly pouring a sixth bucket of water into Adam. Now overflowing with the fluid Spirit of Life, Adam stood up and began dancing around. God smiled, knowing the secret of success, and ever after saturated every human child to overflowing with fluid spirit.

Water is an essential source of life for living things. Water constitutes more than 60% of your body, 90% of your blood, and 80% to 90% of your muscles. Without water to drink you would die within ten days or less, depending on your activity and the temperature. So let water be your new image of your indispensable soul.

The next time you drink a glass of water, take a shower or bath, or watch it rain, prayerfully ponder water as a vital image of your soul. Consciously use water as a soul symbol, so that even a simple drink of water will become a moist prayer of remembrance of your inner self.

My Dear Friend,

Several days have lapsed since I wrote the last Prayer Note. As you know, I'm enthusiastic about the fascinating history of words. I awoke one morning contemplating the family history of the English word "soul." It occurred to me that in these notes I have frequently referred to that word while taking its meaning for granted.

Inspired in my exploration, I discovered that our word "soul" comes to us through Old English, and originally from the Germanic word *saiwalo,* which literally means "from the sea." My delight snowballed as my beloved dictionary continued to explain that this word arose from an ancient Germanic belief that souls originated in and returned to the sea! So it seems that our rather improbable Genesis tale of Adam being waterlogged with the gift of his soul had hidden primordial Germanic roots. This legend is a resurfacing in our age of another ancient spiritual tradition about the nature of the soul.

Water as a soul image is not part of our Jewish, Christian and Moslem traditions, where breath is seen as the source of the soul. Yet the sea is so sensual and water so tangible. It's easy to envision those ancient ones of Northern Europe having a tactile experience of the sea as sacred, as the source of their souls and their final destination. Perhaps they even prayed, "Water you are, and to water you shall return."

My hope is that this reflection will encourage you to contemplate even plain water as sacred. Besides being the element of Jewish purification baths and Christian Baptism, could not water, even in its daily use, become a sacramental? If you are a Catholic Christian, you might also expand your often-unconscious custom of dipping your fingers into the Holy Water font at the entrance of your church with new stimulating possibilities for prayer and soulful awareness.

My Dear Friend,

Whenever we have lunch, I notice that you always drink water with your meals. Since you are such a fan of water, I have a new title for you: a fountain follower of the Master. Describing himself as a fountain of living water, he said that those who drank of his water would never be thirsty again. He went on to say that those who quenched their thirst with his living water would themselves become fountains bubbling up with endless life.

Fountains, like those seen in Rome, can be masterpieces of beauty, yet if they are not alive with splashing water they have a lifeless beauty. Regardless of how handsome the body, its beauty is also lifeless unless the soul is bubbling up out of it. Neglect of the inner spring of living water results in dry fountains, parched personalities and arid identities.

Wherever the Master went, the thirsty crowded around him to drink deeply and be refreshed by the spray from the surging overflow of his soul life. Those who were thirsty then are the same thirsty today who yearn to drink of the water of acceptance and understanding, to be quenched by friendship and affection, soaked in the spirit of freedom and drenched in joyfulness. By a holy bath, you have been dedicated as a fountain — so, be one! To be an overflowing fountain requires daily digging deeper into your inner well of spirit. Prayer is the shovel — use it.

Jesus again referred to himself as life-giving water when

he said that if anyone believed in him "rivers of living water" would flow out of that person. A fountain is stationary, fixed in a particular place, while a river is dynamically ambulatory. A river is, thus, a source of fertility and life everywhere it flows. What an awesome image of your vocation!

Today, be a river of spirit water bringing freshness, life and delight to all with whom you come in contact. Let your soul gurgle outward freely to irrigate those made barren by a drought of hope, causing them to come alive. From your surplus soul water, by your unguarded openness, invite the dour and dry to eagerly fill their empty canteens with your soul's elixir of joy.

As a fountain follower, your major work this day is to be refreshing, revitalizing water.

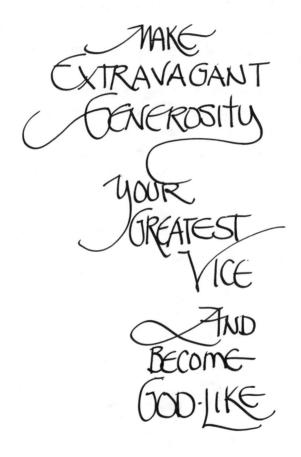

MAKE
EXTRAVAGANT
GENEROSITY

YOUR
GREATEST
VICE

AND
BECOME
GOD·LIKE

My Dear Friend,

In our recent luncheon visit, we discussed our use of hands in prayer. The Koran says that God is closer than the vein in your neck. What a beautiful invitation to pray. In fact, it suggests a new way to pray: Begin by placing your first and second fingers on your throat's jugular vein. Linger there as you feel the vigorous throbbing of life within you. Praying with your fingers on your jugular vein can be a sensual affirmation that God is not distant or remote but is pulsating within you. I personally have found this prayer gesture to be extraordinarily affirming of my core spiritual and intellectual belief, and so I present this practice for your consideration.

God is life. What better way to be mindful of the nearness of the Presence than to actually feel it vibrating on your fingertips? To gain the attention of God, your intimate Beloved, does not require bellowing prayers, clanging bells or thunderous pipe organ preludes. A silent sensual touch can profoundly awaken you to God's perpetual attention to you and your needs.

Besides being an excellent preface to any prayer, this tactile throat prayer gesture is useful whenever you are in need of God's presence. Use your Jugular Prayer whenever you feel yourself sinking deeper and deeper in the quicksand of an argument or trapped in a no-win discussion — or in any difficult encounter.

My Dear Friend,

This Note picks up on another dimension of the Jugular Prayer proposed in my previous note. I separated the two reflections in the hope that before you read this entry you will have had some experience with that two-finger prayer gesture. Besides being a tactile prayer expression, Jugular Prayer can also be a critical digital device in your spiritual espionage. Indeed, it is a secret agent prayer. The Master Spy gave his disciples, his comrade spies for God, a concise code for behavior that would never draw any attention to them. All good secret agents blend into the culture and never tip their hands as to their true identity.

"Shhh," the Master might have said, placing a finger to his lips, "keep your spirituality secret." He laid out his whole code for his secret agents in the sixth chapter of St. Matthew's Manual of Instruction. I can hear him saying:

"When you give alms, do so secretly so that your left hand doesn't know what your right is doing. In other words, in charity be underhanded.

"Do not pray in public, for it will expose you. Pray covertly and keep it brief. Your stealthy God who loves to be secret knows everything you need—so abbreviate your prayers.

"If you want to fast, cleverly disguise yourself as joyously feasting. Hide your acts of penance. Do not decorate your faces with signs of repentance, for remember that you are clandestine agents of God."

Written in this chapter with invisible ink are other admonitions: Do not wear halos. Do not wear distinctive clothing revealing your identity. Do not adorn yourself with jewelry or signs associated with the Master. If you must use symbols, use only covert, mysterious ones. Avoid all God-talk except in your spy cell meetings. In public do not carry your secret agent training manual containing the sayings of the Master Spy. Blend in, yet at the same time be unceasing in your underground activities to overthrow the Anti-Kingdom.

Typically, Jesus kept secret his — and God's — reason why we are to practice a hidden holiness. Perhaps the unexplained reason is the powerful influence of the invisible. Soul power flows effortlessly out of you and impacts the negativity you encounter. The invisible is potently influential — much more so than surface capacities. When tempted to be overt in your spirituality, redouble your covert confidence in your soul power.

A Jugular Prayer expresses a fidelity to the Master of Hidden Holiness. You can use it in the crowded shopping mall, at your desk, and driving home from work. Prayer rituals and postures have great value since they influence the mind and heart. Yet as one of God's secret agents, you need not drop to your knees or piously fold your hands to pray. By innocently placing your two fingers on your jugular vein, you can silently pray to your God throbbing at your fingertips.

My Dear Friend,

Recently I've been reflecting on how paradoxical prayer is for me. Spirited prayers do not begin in the heart or on your lips as much as they emerge out of your soul. The enigma is that exuberant prayer has its beginning in a Sonora soul. The Sonora desert of Northern Mexico and Southern Arizona is an arid image of the parched soulscape, where real prayer can begin. The poet-psalmist sings about this condition in Psalm 63, "O God, for you I long! My soul thirsts for you like a land parched, lifeless and without water." Recall my previous Notes about the soul as water — God bringing Adam to life by pouring buckets of water into him and Jesus' words about being fountains and rivers of living water.

Healthy, then, is a parched soul that can acknowledge the need to be replenished by God with the source of life. Sage is the shriveled soul that knows how easily it becomes dehydrated by being chronically busy. Keeping the well of the soul from not drying up requires being replenished by the divine underground river and by daily prayer showers. Arid souls are infertile, like inhospitable deserts, incapable of nourishing your spiritual powers.

Good prayer is not piously plodding through an obligation. Rather, pray with a lover's longing, "O God, how I long for you. How my soul yearns for you. Like a thirsty traveler in the Sonora or the Sahara who craves a clear flowing stream of water, so do I crave you." Yet the experience of being truly thirsty is rare in our "all-needs-met-and-no-privation" Western World. Other than the extremely sick or dying, or long-distance runners, who of us knows the parched taste of authentic thirst? Being physically thirsty and hungry is prayerful preparation for all authentic expressions of your soul, which is constantly dependent upon God, even to pray.

Ponder nature's miracle of a sudden spring rain that can transform a once-parched desert with colorful, luxurious blooms. Before you pray, begin by spending some Sonora-Sahara desert time with your soul, and then do a rain-dance prayer.

My Dear Friend,

Your soul's radar is constantly scanning the familiar in everything you see, hear, feel and taste for indications of the invisible, imperishable Presence. While our soul has never lost its ability to detect the divine reality within all things, we often fail to consult our souls, especially with regard to that which is familiar to us.

In the Book of Wisdom the inspired writer says of God:

> For you love all things that are
> and loath nothing you have made,
> for anything you hated
> you would not have created....
> You spare all things...
> for your imperishable spirit
> is in all things.

How wondrous are the implications of those seven holy words, "...your imperishable spirit is in all things." Those words can mystify your logical mind but can also stir aflame your mystic soul.

Your soul is, indeed, that of a mystic since it was specifically designed to experience the Imperishable Mystery in all things. Mysticism is nothing more than directly experiencing the Divine Presence. Your soul has been invested with a passionate desire to make visible the invisible. Your ever-alert soul shouts to you, "Look over there...and there...and there. Do you not see? Take off your shoes; prostrate yourself in adoration." Soul-deaf by routine and blinded by the familiar, we hurry past God while rushing to church, synagogue or mosque so as to be with God.

While being handicapped with regard to soul-sight and hearing, mystics still attempt to treat all things with adoration and reverence.

Indeed, a solitary hermit could spend an entire lifetime pondering the countless epiphanies that affirm those seven words and would still never come close to grasping their implications.

"Your imperishable spirit is in all things." Busy-with-daily-life mystics like yourself would do well to memorize those seven words. Use them as your mantra; recite them as your handicapped prayer of sightless-seeing as you see, hear and touch the Hidden Divine everywhere in God's Enchanted Kingdom.

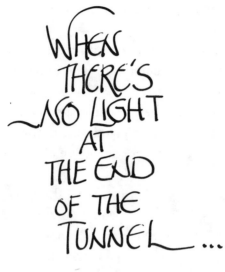

WHEN
THERE'S
NO LIGHT
AT
THE END
OF THE
TUNNEL ...

START
DIGGING
LIKE
HELL.

My Dear Friend,

Our powerlessness to do anything without the continuing assistance of God is unquestionable, yet you and I daily behave as if this is not true. We quickly move from task to task, cocksure of our abilities to accomplish them without any help from God.

Consider a short prayer of only four words that's borrowed from a courtroom of law: "So help me, God." This traditional conclusion to an oath of truthfulness by a witness, which includes placing the right hand on a bible, can be an ideal prayer reminder. This short "hands on" prayer has great possibilities for awakening you to an essential and undeniable reality: your absolute dependence upon God.

To help awaken you to reality, you might try beginning each task to which you put your hand by saying, "So help me, God." Use that four-word prayer as you grasp the steering wheel of your car, finger the keyboard of your computer, or place the kitchen pot on the stove for the evening's meal of chili. "So help me, God" is both prayer and self-talk as you announce your absolute dependence upon God.

"So help me, God" is the prayerful plea of the needy. "So help me, God" is a cry from the depths. "So help me, God" is the cry of the impotent. "So help me, God" is prayer testimony to tell the whole truth by living the whole Truth and nothing but the Truth.

My Dear Friend,

At the very end of our last visit you asked, "Can one be a contemporary contemplative, a modern mystic, right in the midst of a busy lifestyle?" We lacked time then to explore your question, so I send my thoughts in this Note.

Even in the busiest lives it takes only a few seconds to contemplate the Invisible. Yet those who practice this prayer of the eyes are true contemplatives. Usually contemplation is considered an act of intently thinking or meditating on something — often for hours at a time. Its original meaning, however, is a special way of seeing. Contemplating is gazing attentively, as when your eyes frame the viewed object in such a way as to see only it. Gazing implies far more than glancing. Most of seeing is glancing, where your eye looks briefly at something and then is deflected off to something else.

A true Prayer of the Eye is rare. It is difficult because, like most of us, you've forgotten your primordial vocation. The result is that your normal vision is a combination of glancing and a panoramic viewing of unfolding, continuously changing scenes. Contemplatives, on the other hand, are mystic gazers, for gazing means seeing with wonder and expectation. Don't let the word mystic intimidate you; it only refers to one who beholds reality from the perspective of the soul. Indeed, your vocation to be a mystic was seeded in you at your soul's conception. The divine insemination implanted a mystical embryo containing the soul's second-sight, which is necessary for you to be a visionary.

The spiritual life is a birthing room where your Gynecologist God is present as you labor to give birth. Along with your other exercises today, practice the Prayer of the Eye. Tether the eyes of your soul to those of your body, and then gaze prayerfully upon whatever is directly in front of you. Gazing is a three-act play. First, look with wonder, with holy awe, at the beauty, design, and rich or subtle coloring of the object of your gazing. Second, look with expectation, with adorational anticipation of the appearance of the Invisible One who saturates all that encircles you, seen and unseen. Act Three can be viewed from several possible vantage points. Viewed one way, the anticipated doesn't appear, leaving the viewer disappointed. Viewed from another angle, the Invisible does appear, at a terrifying cost to the viewer. Viewed in yet a third way, the viewer, by gazing, is God-filled and so explodes with joyful delight.

Contemplating the Invisible involves looking twice; it is sight without seeing — viewing with reverence. Such frequent eye exercises are prayerful enhancements that magnify the Presence in your life. Practice this prayerful gazing; still your mind and look a second time at anything or anyone in the field of your vision. With faith-sight, realize that you are gazing upon the Invisible One within the skin-deep visible.

Look with loving adoration and with wonder, and then hold your breath as you apprehend the awesome truth that the Invisible One is also fondly gazing back at you.

My Dear Friend,

In a previous note I talked about your vocation to be a mystic and visionary. Visionaries can be prophetic persons whose insights are ahead of their time; they can also be fantasy dreamers whose ideals are impractical and too idealistic. To nurture your mystical visionary vocation, God has given you the holy avocation of being an *incubator*.

An incubator is a controlled device that provides temperature and atmospheric conditions ideal for hatching eggs or sustaining premature babies, insulating them from life-threatening circumstances. As a disciple of Jesus, yours is the destiny of sheltering the premature dream of God's reign from the many menacing environmental forces of the Anti-Kingdom.

Jesus delivered the divine dream "in the fullness of time," according to God's timetable, but it was premature as far as the world was concerned. That dream of a new social order based on peace and justice, love and compassion, is still alive today. That dream, which was pregnant with such high ideals, is still viable because of the legions of holy incubators who have kept it alive throughout the centuries. In apostolic succession, you are to be a walking incubator, carrying God's dream that must be safeguarded within the proper temperature and atmosphere in order to survive. The prayer of such incubators is "May your kingdom come, in me, here on earth, as it is has already come in heaven."

Hope is essential to generate the needed warm temperature and loving atmosphere required to ensure that the forces of cynicism, greed and violence do not suck the life out of the divine dream a-birthing in you. Hope breeds anticipation. You pray hope-saturated warmth into your environment with every positive statement you make about people and the world. Each time you affirm the good work of another, you are engaged in incubator prayer. Not returning violence for violence or injury for injury, loving your enemies, and lending without expecting a return are among the incubator acts proposed by the Dreamer Jesus. Whenever you perform any of these idealistic deeds commanded by the Master, not as unreachable ideals but as part of a living moral code, you are living as a visionary incubator.

By such Godlike deeds performed with love and hope, the divine dream you carry within you grows, and the world comes one step closer to believing the Gospel is possible.

My Dear Friend,

This note continues the last reflection, encouraging you to see yourself as a holy incubator. An incubator can also be a controlled temperature and humidity (or, in our case, humility) apparatus for multiplying microcosmic cell cultures of growths such as the flu virus. It may seem strange to ask you to become this kind of incubator, yet the kingdom of God is spread like the flu virus, which is one of evolution's most successful stories. Among the reasons for the survival of this virus is its capacity for constantly mutating under the influence of the host's DNA. Thus, each year a new flu vaccine is created to combat this ever-adapting virus.

Hope heats the protective shelter within you in which the contagion of Christ thrives. Be patient, for like a virus this holy infection spreads to one person at a time. It also acts like a flu virus in that it doesn't always immediately manifest itself; so, again, be hopeful and patient. Your contagion may take months or even years before it becomes active.

By maintaining your hope-quenched heart, you continue to perpetuate the virus of Christianity. As one of its infected agents, you spread this divine virus everywhere you go. Live each day consciously, prayerfully inflecting as many people as possible with hope, joy and love. Contaminate every place you visit; pollute every project with hope and joy.

And when you look back over your life's work of being a Dream-carrier and fear that the dark forces of the Anti-Kingdom have won, redouble your hope. Be full of hope, for the ever-mutating virus of God's love will again refashion itself in another new expression for which there is no known cure.

P.S. The Chinese have a saying, "Keep a green branch in your heart, and for sure a songbird will come." In our case that songbird is the Spirit, whose song in the predawn darkness signals the arrival of God's eternal spring. I encourage you, and me, to keep our branches green.

IN WATER TOO PURE THERE ARE NO fISH.

A CHINESE SAYING

My Dear Friend,

In your last letter you told me about your friend who seems uptight and frustrated, and how whenever you attempt to discuss her problem your suggestions are rejected. You wondered what I would suggest.

I might propose trying the Bartender Prayer or *sbottonarsi* (sbot-uh-NARE-see), an Italian word meaning "to open up." Like many of us, your friend keeps her feelings all bottled up inside her. What she needs isn't a conversation about her problems; she needs an uncorking that will allow her to open up and release the agitation bubbling up inside.

Uncorking is bartender's work, whether for people or bottles. And when dealing with friends, the corkscrew of choice can be the simple expression, "You look very tense and upset." If your friend responds and begins to pour out his or her issues, you only need to be a good listener. Each time you allow others to release whatever is pent up within, you are praying the Bartender's Prayer. It can happen that your friends pop open the cork themselves and begin to pour out their difficulties. When this happens, know that an hour spent simply in listening is an hour spent in prayer. The great Protestant theologian Paul Tillich wrote about "the love that listens." What more beautiful way to love another than by trying to listen with understanding and compassion.

The Italian *sbottonarsi* is a good introduction to this Bartender Prayer since it literally suggests "unbuttoning." In American slang, having our feelings bottled up is called being "uptight." It's an appropriate phrase for having so tightly buttoned oneself up that one can hardly breathe. Those restrained in such psychic straightjackets are eager to be unbuttoned and usually need outside help to be released. The best way to help unfasten someone from such complex buttons is by asking the right questions in a loving and gentle way. Good bartenders, counselors and spiritual directors all know that asking the right questions is far superior to giving the right answers.

When someone is burdened with inner turmoil and personal problems, the modern tendency in our culture is to direct that person to a professional, since the ordinary person feels unqualified to help. Resist the temptation to do this automatically, and remember that bartenders hear more confessions than priests do! Neighbors are approached more frequently than psychologists for emotional help. By their willingness just to listen, these nonprofessional persons have the power to heal the afflicted of soul.

The first requirement of Bartender Prayer is a willingness to listen compassionately, without prejudice or the need to make a moral judgment. Do not be concerned about your lack of professional training. In your poverty of professional skill, silently call upon the Spirit of Wisdom to supply everything you need, especially the grace of nonjudgmental listening. When you are called upon to practice the "love that listens," do not be concerned about your inability to know the right questions to ask; trust that the Great Listener to all the sufferings of humanity will supply you with the right words when you ask.

This "love that listens" is truly a triple blessing. The first blessing is the healing liberation of the afflicted person who has released what is buried deeply within. Often by this act of emancipation, the solutions the person seeks also slowly surface. The second blessing is that by your tender, soulful listening you will receive what the Master promised: By showing compassion, you will be shown compassion. Thirdly, admitting you don't know the right questions to ask is an acknowledgment of your state of poverty, and as the Teacher also said: Blessed are the poor, for God shall enrich them.

My Dear Friend,

Since my Prayer Note about replacing a "subtraction spirituality" with a "superlative spirituality," I'm sure you've wondered about the value of practicing any spiritual disciplines or self-denial. I'd like to suggest that there are many practices of self-sacrifice that can strengthen your spiritual life and feed your soul. For example, the Sacrifice of the Tongue is one of those invisible disciplines that reaps rich rewards for all who engage in this priestly ritual. Unlike daily sacrifices, this ritual is used only in those urgent times when words of criticism, disagreement, anger and impatience are beginning to take shape on your tongue. In the micro-seconds of their forming, they are first tasted on our tongue with an appetizing eagerness to be spoken. It is at this critical moment that you need to perform the Sacrifice of the Tongue.

Begin the ritual by gently gripping the tip of your tongue with your upper and lower teeth and softly squeezing them together, thus restraining your tool of speech. This unspoken prayer of tongue retention will prevent you from speaking. The next step is to swallow your intended critical or negative words. On certain occasions this may require having to gulp down the unspoken remark like a big pill or a large piece of unchewed steak. Only when the impulse to express whatever your soul has judged to be inappropriate disappears should you gently release your tongue. Yet do so with an inner smile of gratitude, for in the act of silencing your tongue, your soul has grown.

I referred to this sacrifice as a priestly ritual because over five hundred years ago a variation of it was practiced by Aztec priests in Mexico. As a sacred penance the priests pierced their tongues with mescal cactus thorns, causing them to bleed. This bleeding tongue ritual symbolized the great sacrifice of human hearts at the Great Pyramid in Tenochtitlan. The sacred offering of hundreds — even thousands — of human hearts was the core ritual of their sun-renewing sacrifices.

This Prayer of the Tongue sacramentalizes the old folk saying, "Bite your tongue." Shakespeare made use of this graphic idiom for refraining from negative speech in his play *Henry VI*: "So York must sit and fret and bite his tongue." An even older and more appropriate saying that describes this ritual comes from around 1387 in Chaucer's *The Tale of Melibus*, "Thee is better hold thy tongue still, than for to speak."

I conclude this Prayer Note by daring to paraphrase the great Chaucer, "Thee is blessed to hold thy tongue still, than for to speak."

My Dear Friend,

As you scale the Mountain of God, know that the spoken word can only take you so far. To successfully reach the summit you must go the rest of the way in silence. Spoken prayers, being measurable in length and devotion, seem superior — if your yardstick is official public worship. As walking is often considered an inefficient means for reaching a destination, so silence is often deemed unproductive in reaching God. This hasty evaluation leads the majority of seekers to attempt to ascend the Mountain of God using spoken prayers as their all-terrain, four-wheel-drive vehicles.

The Prayer of Silence requires great faith since it lacks an odometer, speedometer or thermometer. Yet even though you may lack a tangible gauge for the progress of your prayer, your confidence in the Prayer of Stillness can be greatly advanced when you consider that silence is a particular form of speech. In Jewish mysticism, for example, we find the contradictory expression, "silent speech," referring to a prayer known as the royal path to God. The divine economy of this two-dimensional prayer is illustrated in an old Jewish proverb: "Speech is worth a penny, silence is worth two."

Fasting, that age-old spiritual practice, has its place in twenty-first century spirituality. Traditional religious fasting involves abstaining from food on certain days and during holy seasons. The kind of fast needed in our ever-chatting culture, however, is a fasting from speech. The frequent practice of abstaining from talking is a Seminary of Silent Speech. In that holy school you will learn a most fruitful art for your prayer and for your daily life.

A playful, prayer paradox is hidden away in our English word "fast." Its first meaning isn't abstaining from food; rather, it means swiftly, instantly, rapidly. So when your prayer is Silent Speech, you'll travel to God lickety-split.

My Dear Friend,

I appreciate your concern about the effectiveness of your prayer, especially when it comes to praying for those who have asked you to remember them in prayer. Have you ever considered your astonishing capacity to pray backwards? Prayer-in-Reverse is possible since it exists in Divine Reality, which is free of the boundaries of time and space. All prayer is in the present moment, regardless of when you pray, since God always exists in the Eternal Now.

I've found it fruitful as well as adventuresome when I've prayed backwards for the needs of my friends. When asked to pray for the successful outcome of a particular situation on a specific day, I have continued to pray for that person's need for days afterwards while awaiting some word from them. In the case of communication by mail, this backwards praying may continue for an extended period of time.

Perhaps, like myself, you have sometimes forgotten to pray for someone's intention on the specified day. Do not be overly disturbed even when the day of note has come and gone, for you can still pray for the person. Whenever you remember your prayer promise, even if it is days afterwards, you can intentionally send your prayer backwards in time to the place and hour of need. I assure you that God will answer your prayer, surrounding such persons with the Divine Presence to assist them in their time of need.

(Paradoxically, I've found that recognizing the value of backwards prayer has increasingly helped me to be prayerfully present right at the critical moment someone has requested my prayerful solidarity.)

While prayer is usually reserved for needs in the present or future, why should it not also be exercised in the past? Why limit God's activity to our restricted time and space dimensions? Why harness your imagination regarding the scope of your soul's powers to pray historically? Of course, praying backwards requires faith, a wholehearted trust in prayer's ability to be effective anywhere at any time. Indeed, all praying requires deep faith, a wholehearted trust.

Still, do not be concerned if your faith in prayer seems small, because even a tiny mustard-seed-sized faith can be tremendously powerful. The ceiling of prayer's potential was raised sky high when Jesus said, "If you pray with faith — with a loyal fidelity in me — your prayer will have the power to move mountains." And, I might add, the power to move clocks backwards.

My Dear Friend,

Like you, I regard a time of recovery from illness, whether great or small, as an opportunity to rejoice. As well as a time to celebrate, I'd like to suggest that it's also a prime opportunity for prayer. So when you recover, don't throw away your emptied medicine bottles! After recovery from any affliction, give your old medicine bottles a place of honor on your bathroom sink as a disguised prayer shrine. Let it become a visual bell calling you to prayer: the prayer of gratitude for your health, which is among the most taken-for-granted gifts.

Your empty prescription container is a silent gong that can awaken your mind and quicken your soul to pray a silent "Thank You" for your gift of wellness. I've found such thanksgiving prayers to be contagious. These prayers of appreciation can be downright infectious, circulating gratitude throughout your body as quickly as the flu spreads. You might be grateful for legs that walk without difficulty, for arms and joints that maneuver without pain or for internal organs that effortless and efficiently work day and night. Your thankfulness may extend out to embrace your healthy relationships, your profitable labors, your gifts and talents, and on and on.

So, even when illness is far away from your conscious concern, consider practicing this form of a visual prayer reminder. Having visible uninhabited medication containers can be "good medicine" that enables a healthy, energetic soul. A lack of a daily tonic of gratitude results in an anemic soul, which, in turn, contributes to a physical sense of listlessness. A grateful soul, on the other hand, is vibrant and animated and so permeates your body with zest and with an enjoyment of a life littered with gifts.

My Dear Friend,

I appreciate your sense of sometimes feeling flat and arid in your prayer life. In fact, today my own devotion is taking the form of Cactus Prayer, for I just don't feel like praying. Whatever the cause, whether a restless night, a tired, overloaded life, or whatever the reason, this morning my soul is desert dry. My soul's lamp of devotion is usually enkindled by some spiritual reading, which acts as a preface to my prayers. This morning, my eyes aren't hungry for the printed word. So I attempted wordless scripture, sitting and gazing out my window at the 10,000 living words of God in creation. Even this usually rich experience, however, is arid of inspiration today.

I feel the nudge of routine saying, "Your day *should* begin with prayer. You know how critical that ritual is to your soul-life." Yet I resist the nudge. Then my soul feels the irritating pricking of cactus needles, "Edward, you *should* pray, regardless of how you feel, how devoid you are of devotion, for love is more than a feeling. Love is fidelity. So begin your prayers."

Instead, I decide to bivouac in the barren wasteland as an atheist and not pray. However, slowly and surprisingly, in the midst of my desert there bubbles up a spring of fresh peace. I am enveloped in a serenity of soul that seems to evolve from simply allowing the desert to be the desert. As I cease desiring any miraculous spring shower to cause my arid wasteland to bloom, it paradoxically begins to open out to an enchanted landscape of tranquility.

Surprised again in prayer! This time by a minor miracle whose source seems to be embracing the cactus of my inability to pray easily or naturally. This miracle is, indeed, a sand-dune sunrise — it's the dawning realization that my very longing to pray is itself prayer. Then that miracle spawns another — an electrical surge of hope and consolation from the awareness that even if I don't pray at all today, my soul is still ceaselessly praying.

I pray you will find peace through this reflection on the graces found in "not praying."

My Dear Friend,

> As a follower of the Way,
> a superlative way to pray
> is to go out of your way.

You are not alone when you feel a tension between your life of prayer and the many demands present in the rest of your life. Yet those two aspects of your existence need not be at odds. The short verse that began this Note speaks of the prayerfulness of every detour you make in order to do something for another. Jesus could have called it the Samaritan superlative way to follow his Way of Love. I recently came upon this type of prayer in Frederic and Mary Ann Brussat's book *Spiritual Literacy*. They quoted the Quaker writer, Richard Foster: "(When) we stretch ourselves on behalf of others (it) is a prayer of action." Among his examples of this type of prayer are scrimping to get your children through school, sharing your car by giving others a lift, keeping up with your correspondence, and making one more telephone call at night when you're tired.

Foster's idea of extending yourself on behalf of others as a form of prayer lit up my soul like a Christmas tree. I began to be conscious of how whenever I have performed this kind of action I have been praying. Previously, I might have considered such an action more as a "should" than a rich possibility for prayer. I now experience it not as a Christian duty but as a delightful way to pray always.

I've named them Samaritan Prayers, based on Jesus' parable encouraging us to practice loving our neighbor by going out of our way. I also call this form Stretching Prayer or Detour Prayer, depending on the nature of the situation. But most of all, I call myself *elated* since this discovery of yet another way to "pray ceaselessly."

You engage in Samaritan Prayer at those times when you extend yourself to respond to letters you've received, each time you send a thank-you note or remember an anniversary with a greeting card. And when you detour from your tightly scheduled day to respond with a generosity of time and attention to someone in need, know that this "wasted time" is time spent praying.

The next time any circumstance invites you to make a detour in your well-planned day to extend yourself for another, may you find delight in going out of your way as a most precious prayer of the Way.

My Dear Friend,

Movie stars are our culture's icons of beauty. It's easy to long for our faces to be like those of Hollywood stars. Yet do not envy Hollywood beauty, for yours is the awesome beauty of Holywork. Beautiful is your soul, the handsome and holy work of God. Each of us has an inner face, which Zen calls "our original face" or "our true face." Unfortunately, in this life there are no mirrors capable of inner-reflection, and so you are never able to see your stunningly beautiful soul face. However, others can, and they do whenever you reside in the State of Forgetfulness of Self. On those occasions when you can forget about yourself in the process of caring for another, the inner beauty of your soul radiates outward, transfiguring your countenance.

Instead of *face*, I intentionally use the word *countenance*, because of its rich legacy that speaks to self-forgetfulness. The Latin parent word *continentia* means restraint; what is being held back is your obsessively self-serving ego. By divine design you have a primitive inner drive to be selfish so you can properly care for your physical survival. Yet restraint is critical for disengaging this primal driving impulse so you can respond to the needs of others. By divine design you also have another impelling inner power, which was implanted at soul birth to drive you to become divine-like. When this soul power is activated, you can redirect your response from your own needs to those of another. Whenever this happens, your face experiences a transparency. And the more often it occurs, the more fully your beautiful hidden soul face transfigures your outward countenance.

Don't attempt to catch a glimpse of this inner beauty by sneaking a look in the mirror as you pretend to be selfless. This miraculous transfiguration occurs only in a graced moment of forgetfulness, which paradoxically also leads to remembering. In that remembrance two realities are recalled. The first is Christ's words that you love and care for him whenever you love others and care for their needs. This reality embraces the mystery that Christ's needs are also the needs of others. The second, and often surprising, remembrance is that this mystery is true for you as well. That which you call your self is constantly united with the Greater Self, the Soul of all created beings, enabling you to realize that whatever you do to another you are doing to yourself.

In this Note I guess I am strangely encouraging you to find great delight in exposing yourself in public! I don't mean the criminal act but the graced act — the act of exposing your beautiful inner-self. In the process may you find joy in the hidden law of our inner drives, which says that switching from Survival Drive to Soul Drive can be almost effortless. In fact, it requires less and less exertion when after each visit to the State of Self-Forgetfulness you rejoice with profound gratitude for the opportunity to become beautiful.

My Dear Friend,

As you deepen your commitment to the path of prayer, one word that sums up your goal in life is *mahatma*. This Sanskrit word from India means "large or great soul." It is commonly used for wise and holy persons like Mohandas Gandhi.

It is an alien word in our Christian vocabulary, perhaps because we don't often view the soul as being capable of growth. The heart, on the other hand, since it is regarded as the center of our emotions, consciousness and spiritual life, is perceived as a growing, developing organ. A loving person is called "bighearted," and someone lacking compassion is "hard-hearted." As the critical organ for pumping blood throughout the body, your heart is the symbolic center of emotional life and feelings. Your soul, on the other hand, being the seamless animating principle of your entire person, lacks such localization.

While your symbolic spiritual images have been strongly shaped by scripture and tradition, I'd like to propose a spiritual exercise to help you become more conscious of the inner reality known as your soul. Consider exchanging the word *soul* for *heart* in the following common phrases: It broke my soul; I learned the poem by soul; have a soul; you stole my soul; she wears her soul on her sleeve; his soul is in the right place; with all my soul; with half a soul; a soul attack; a broken soul.

Prayer is generally viewed as an activity of the heart and mind. In fact, the classical definition of prayer is lifting up one's heart and mind to God. Yet praying from either the heart or the mind compartmentalizes prayer, which is an integral human act. When you pray, consider frequently substituting the pronoun "I" and the terms "mind" and "heart" with that of "soul." Practicing these two substitution exercises will both vitalize and integrate, and will help you experience your prayers as originating from a deeper place within you. Moreover, the more you involve your soul in daily life and prayer, the more it will grow toward being a *mahatma.*

As Jesus warns us, it is hazardous to your soul to seek to become renowned as a holy person. So follow the wisdom of the Master and place the adjective "secret" in front of the term *mahatma* as you make it your daily aspiration. Yet be a *mahatma* you must — if you are to progress on the path of prayer.

Besides the above exercises in substitution, your soul will also grow whenever you engage in prayer, silent reflection, meditation, silence and solitude. Your soul is enlarged when you read scripture and books on spirituality, along with the time you spend among God's living words of creation. Perhaps the choicest cultivation of a beautiful *mahatma* is by generous loving and unselfish service to others. Throughout all your daily activities keep this image of *mahatma* before you.

My Dear Friend,

In the midst of your feelings of being scattered and fragmented in your spiritual pursuit, consider this ancient rule: "Wherever the heart goes, the rest of you will soon follow in its wake." Whenever you send your heart ahead of you to undertake some project, your mind, will and emotions will play follow the leader. So, when you find yourself faced with a seemingly impossible task, it is wise not to ask your mind what you should do; instead, send your heart bravely off alone to tackle the task.

I prefer to adjust one word in that ancient wisdom — to replace "heart" with "soul." Instead of fretting about how you might achieve the impossible, passionately send your soul off into that unachievable project, then sit and wait patiently.

As if ashamed to be left fearfully behind, sinking in a quicksand pool of distrust, you'll find that your emotions, mind and will power will arise to be where your soul is already encamped. Indeed, the mind, being ever analytical, quickly dismisses as foolish and impossible whatever appears illogical or impractical. Your will, in turn, tends to be handicapped since it waits for orders from your mind. Your emotions, until grounded in resolve, are prone to avoid going where angels fear to tread. However, your soul, being eternally intertwined with its Source, knows that with God, "all things are possible," as the angel told Mary of Nazareth.

Indeed, the Kingdom of God is the Realm of the Impossible, where enemies are to be loved instead of hated and those who injure you are to be repaid with blessings rather than brutality. The Book of God's Reign is full of such seemingly unreachable requirements. While challenging, they are not impossible.

The next time you feel that fate, life or God has given you some impossible mission, don't be paralyzed by its doomed appearance. Instead, sprightly send off your soul as a pioneer to homestead the undoable project. Your soul, being a born follower of God, goes where angels may fear to go, but it's where God has already gone and calls us to follow. So with holy confidence send your soul as a scout to begin your impossible task, and I assure you, the rest of you will soon follow.

P.S. Today you will undoubtedly come face to face with one of the numerous "impossible" Gospel challenges. When you do, simply recall this Prayer Note and "send in your soul."

My Dear Friend,

Do you know that at this moment you are praying the ancient prayer of hieroglyphics? That word, which means "sacred marks or pictographs," was used by Egyptians for the art of writing. They believed writing to be a sacred gift from the gods.

Our modern world is awash in words — in ink, pencil, paint, neon and especially electronically on our computer screens. Yet words can continue to be gifts from God. Just as with bread and wine, God can consecrate ink and paper as a Sacred Presence to nourish your soul. Besides fostering the growth of your soul, books and articles about spiritual matters can also contain practical answers to your prayers. When you pray for direction in life, be patient and be faithful to your spiritual reading as you attend to the printed word with an open soul.

Your present life situation lends itself to such prayerful reading. In times of doubt or decision or searching for more life, we often long for those once-upon-a-time ancient biblical days when God spoke to people like Abraham, Moses and Jesus. Yet God has not stopped speaking. God speaks to you, encourages and inspires you in countless ways. Perhaps our primary spiritual task is to pay attention and learn how to listen. God communicates to you through the signs of the times and the events of daily life. God speaks to you in the holy words of scripture as well as in the commonplace words in your spiritual reading.

My first exposure to spiritual reading was at age 18 when I went to the seminary. The order of the day required thirty minutes of reading from some book dealing with the spiritual life. The period set aside for this religious exercise was in the afternoon, directly following recreation and sports. While I often fell asleep over my book, it was good training and became a lifelong exercise. I believe this prayerful daily reading should have a central place in every good spiritual practice.

I propose a small ritual to assist you in seeing your time of spiritual reading as the Prayer of Hieroglyphics. Pause before you begin reading, and with your thumb make a small sign of the cross on your forehead and heart. Then as you read, be alert for hidden messages from God addressed personally to you concealed in the words on the page. A good rule for spiritual reading is: Read a little and reflect a lot.

If you desire to have a daily conversation with God, I encourage you to make spiritual reading part of your daily prayer life.

P.S. When I do my spiritual reading, I do so with a pencil and a pad of paper. Then, when an insight arises from the text, I jot it down and expand upon it regarding my personal life.

My Dear Friend,

You ask: "What is the right response to an unanswered prayer?" Pious commentators commonly reply, "Ah, but God does answer every prayer, and sometimes the answer is 'No!'" Conventional wisdom goes on to say the only appropriate response to your unanswered prayer is, "It's God's will. Your will be done."

I propose a different response, based on the advice of Winston Churchill, who said, "Don't take *no* for an answer! Never submit to failure." Jesus agrees. I believe that the Master knew, from personal experience, the bitter taste of his prayers to God not being answered. His excruciatingly soulful prayer in the Garden of Gethsemane was only the last of many such prayerful cries. My belief is based on his parable about the poor widow and the corrupt judge, where he encouraged persistence in petitioning God. The poor widow refused to take *no* for an answer from the crooked judge, and she continued pestering him until he granted her request. Listen to the Master and do what he says. Whenever your prayers come back unfilled, keep prayer-pestering your God, like that poor widow, and God will respond.

The best companion to this Prayer of Knocking Even When the Door Doesn't Open is the prayerful stance of being wide-eyed alert in anticipation of God's novel surprise answer. Jesus promised us that if we pray with faith, our prayers will be granted. He also encouraged us to "Stay awake." So be prepared, for your prayer may be answered in a time and way you would least expect. It might be answered in an even better way than your original request, perhaps better than anything you could have imagined. God loves you passionately and cares deeply for your needs. So remember Jesus' promise: "Seek the kingdom with your whole heart and soul, and everything you need will be given to you."

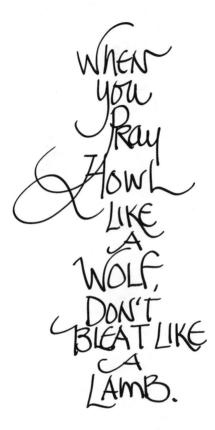

WHEN
YOU
PRAY
HOWL
LIKE
A
WOLF,
DON'T
BLEAT LIKE
A
LAMB.

My Dear Friend,

I have a saying on my desk that I wrote to remind me how to pray: "When you pray, howl like a wolf — don't bleat like a lamb." So I ask: Are you bold enough in what you ask of God in your prayers? Do you have the daring audacity to daily beg to become Godlike, to be a saint? Are you audacious enough to pray with presumption that you might be able to taste the Invisible and savor the Sacred, or do you only pray for practical things?

Consider investing your prayers with more nerve and cheek, with what the Jews call *chutzpah*, pure brazenness. Be gutsy and throw your lukewarm, dishwater tepid prayers down the drain, replacing them with furnace feverish petitions. Then fasten your safety belts, for Jesus promised, "Ask and you shall receive"!

God aches for you to begin to pray for what you truly need. Moreover, you and the world have the same need. What the world needs — even more urgently than peace — is saints. Imagine the impact a hundred living saints would have on the world society. What the church needs more than obedient docile members is contrary prophets. Imagine the effect a hundred living prophets would have on the church. I don't mean oracles of the future but, rather, those who live fully, who live the Gospel, the radical will of God, without compromise. Regardless of your other present needs, what you most deeply need is to become a saint. So pray for it with passion and with *chutzpah*.

My Dear Friend,

Sin is an undeniable reality in life. Who can boast of not falling short in trying to live as a perfect mirror of God? For many, the primary purpose of religion seems to be the avoidance and removal of sin. The Liturgy of the Eucharist begins with a kneeling community plaintively pleading as sinners, "Lord have mercy; Christ have mercy." These poignant pleas to God for mercy are laden with echoes of the pitiful cries of street beggars beseeching a great lord. Those stuck on their knees forget this is only a small part of the liturgy. Moreover, how many of today's worshipers essentially see themselves as sin-laden beggars who must grovel on their knees begging God to pardon them?

While this may sound scandalous, I encourage you to begin to *demand* that God forgive you! The holy theologian St. Gregory of Nyssa, 330-390 C.E., brazenly proposes that you shouldn't get down on your knees weeping to be forgiven! In his *Homilies on the Lord's Prayer*, Gregory says the proper way to address God is with a sense of freedom as a holy citizen of heaven, as a brother/sister of Christ who can boldly assert that God pardon you! The saintly theologian says, "Why...do you go to God crouching with fear like a slave because your conscience pricks you?" He encourages praying not with "abject servility" but with a "holy audacity," boldly calling on God to grant you the pardon to which you are entitled because you have generously forgiven those who have sinned against you! In justice, God owes you forgiveness because you have fulfilled Jesus' requirement to "forgive our trespasses as we forgive those who have trespassed against us."

Gregory goes on to state audaciously, "You want your debts (sins) forgiven by God? Forgive them yourself, and God will ratify it!" What truly good news about your sins and failings! "Forgive them yourself," by granting self-absolution! Recall these words of St. Gregory the next time you feel the prick of a guilt-soaked *should* about going to confession or attending some penance service only to report minor failings or rehash past forgiven sins. The real reason we Christians do not avail ourselves of Jesus' marvelously liberating ritual of pardon is not due to a lack of faith in his words. It is because it is so much easier to confess to a priest or to acknowledge Jesus as our personal savior at a revival than to wholeheartedly forgive those who have caused us pain by sinning against us.

When our ritual of worship requires kneeling, a position of unworthiness, use it as a gesture of self-emptying rather than groveling like a slave before God. Then remind yourself of the awesomely transforming power of your Baptism, which made you one in the Risen Body of the victorious Christ. Those who truly believe in that Easter reality do not kowtow, but stand proudly before God.

Our religious conditioning may lead us to think our baptismal vocation is to witness to Christ in the midst of the secular world. What may be more needed is witnessing to Christ in the midst of our Christian worshipping community.

My Dear Friend,

Your questions about intimacy and God are, indeed, at the heart of a good prayer practice. Unlike the Peanuts' character who said, "I love humanity! It's people I can't stand!" God does not love humanity! God passionately loves each person as an individual, and in a unique and intimate way. As Jesus grew to the full stature of his soul, he became conscious of his uniquely personal love relationship with God, whom he called "Father." He told us that if we asked for anything using his name, it would be given to us. In this instruction is a hidden implication that he himself prayed using his name: "Abba, this is your beloved son Jesus, hear my plea."

I often begin my prayers with, "O gracious and loving God, this is your beloved son Edward. Hear me as I pray for...." I imagine God longs for a chorus of such personalized prayer: "O Ever-Generous Lord, this is Elizabeth...Ruth Ann...Robert...Jackie...James...your highly favored child. I come asking of you...." As you petition God for the needs of others — and all the urgent needs in your life — I encourage you to do so conscious of your unique and very intimate love affair with God.

Traditionally, Christians end their prayers by using the name of Jesus: "We ask this in the name of Jesus, our Lord, who lives and rules with you...." Consider incorporating this ancient tradition into your prayer awareness of your intimate relationship with God by ending your prayers: "I ask this of you in the name of Jesus, my brother and your beloved son, and in my name, _____, also your beloved child."

Among the first fruits of addressing your God in this manner is the cultivation of a wondrous sense of intimacy with your beloved God, from which flows an abiding sense of trust and security.

My Dear Friend,

One of the truly fabulous new inventions in this electronically creative age is e-mail. This form of communication to anywhere in the world is instant and inexpensive. This new electronic courier allows family and friends to send each other the latest news or messages of love and friendship at electrifying speeds. While this was an unimaginable feat only a few years ago, there are more marvels to come! I expect that in the next ten years a newer, faster and more creative messenger will eclipse e-mail.

Rejoice! You don't have to wait ten or twenty years. That courier is already at your fingertips. It's *p-mail*. Prayer-mail requires no equipment and is faster than the speed of light. It is truly free and frees your soul to travel. Prayer has this stunning power since it resides in soul-space as an enterprise of eternity, which is only a parallel universe to ours.

Prayer-mail allows you to send more than a message of love. You can actually send the essence of your love to others. You can p-mail your joyfulness, contentment and the happiness overflowing in your heart as a gift to a friend — or to one clinging onto the edge of despair.

You can use p-mail anytime. Perhaps the prime time for it is when you become conscious of your oversupply of good things and of being saturated with the love of others. Be generous in sharing part of your invisible bounty with others. Only a lack of imagination and a poverty of faith prevent you from sending gifts of your inner self to those you love or with one who feels alienated, alone and abandoned in prison, isolated in a nursing home or stuck in some small, cheap apartment.

Whenever you use the true e-mail, eternity-mail, be prepared for a surprise, for this is mystical mail and unlike any known network of communication and delivery. Once your p-mail gift shipment has been received by the person to whom you sent it, heaven always stamps it *Return to Sender – Tenfold.*

My Dear Friend,

In your present life situation — and whenever you are presented with a problem requiring a new and creative solution — seek the answer to it within yourself, for within you dwells an endlessly innovative God. Believe in that presence as you request a solution to the problem. Then, after saying "amen," fasten your safety belt.

"Ask," the Master taught, "and you shall receive. Pray with confident faith." He could have added, "and with a passionate patience." Step one is to give form to your problem or difficulty by putting it into words within a prayer request. Step two involves praying with confidence that within you resides a perpetually fertile God whose reservoir of imagination is endlessly deep. Wait patiently with the same eager impatience you had as a child on Christmas Eve in anticipation of unwrapping gifts.

God loves surprises, so learn to love being surprised. Take delight in being caught off guard when the gift of your sought-after solution arrives in the midst of taking a shower, reading a magazine or even in the "more likely" moments of meditation. What finer place to be surprised by God than through a divine distraction during meditative prayer? The response to your request may come with such urgency that you are impelled to write it down. A good Rule of Inspiration is: Pray with a pencil by your side.

Millennia ago, God abandoned communicating by

jagged lightening bolts, loud thunderclaps and speaking out of clouds. Silent speech is the preferred language of the Spirit, who cherishes visiting you in those twilight times of musing and daydreaming. At such times your ever-energetic mind is disengaged from practical affairs and your soul-ears are alert. Predawn is another auspicious time for these Spirit Visitations. When possible, treat yourself to lingering in bed during that transition between sleep and wakefulness, and be ready to welcome a surprise visitor.

Here is a prayer for a creative solution:

> O God of Exhilarating Energy,
> Fountain of Creativity,
> Source of All Solutions,
>   who dwells within me,
> I ask with confidence
>   for a gift idea to resolve
>   my problem of _____.
> I wait in patience
>   with the heart of a small child
>   who delights in being surprised.

My Dear Friend,

Warm up your prayers before lifting them up to God. Regardless of how liturgically orthodox your worship might be, God fails to find pleasure in cool-as-chrome prayers. Even lukewarm prayers leave God cold.

Before you offer up any prayer, first preheat your heart furnace to 400 degrees. Then place your prayer of petition, adoration or praise for a few seconds inside that sizzling hot furnace of your heart. Slip on your padded heat-protective oven gloves and carefully remove your broiled prayer. Then lovingly lift it up to God.

As they say in heaven, "There's nothing like a good, hot home-cooked prayer."

A PASSIONATE HEART NEVER AGES.

My Dear Friend,

I'd like to respond to your germinating question of
how to address God in your prayer. The Koran says that
Allah (God) has ninety-nine beautiful names, and supreme
among these are, "Allah, the Compassionate" and "Allah,
the Merciful."

Limited by tradition, Christians generally use only a
handful of names to address God. Habit, even holy habit
and respectful convention, along with a lack of imagination,
can enfeeble our prayers.

I personally have found it useful to enhance my prayers
by adopting the concept of the Koran that God has just one
short of a hundred beautiful names. I try to begin a prayer
by addressing God with a new name tailored to the needs of
my present prayer. The following are some examples.

O My God, *the Ever-Patient*, encompass me in your peace
so I will not act or speak when chafing with impatience.

O My God, *Creator of Order Out of Chaos*, accompany
me as I bring order to my desk...closet...garage...basement...
hectic schedule.

O My God, *Who Delighted in Resting on the Seventh Day*,
assist me to unplug myself so I can be completely
unproductive today by not doing anything of significance or
usefulness.

O My *Divine Source of All Health and Wellness*, come to
the aid of my immune system so it can conquer this virus

I've acquired, and grant your good health to me.

O *My Immeasurably Generous God,* my soul yodels in joyful gratitude that I've found my lost car keys...received this letter from an old friend...been inspired by this article.

O *Beautiful God Who Has Made All in Your Image....*

O *Ever-Changing God Who Revels in the New.....*

O *Unpredictable God Who Thrills in Surprises....*

I encourage you to be creative as you let your new name for God match the occasion of your prayer. When you do this, you will experience a pleasant fresh breeze blowing through your prayer life. Be determined not to slip back into mere habit or pious convention when addressing your Beloved.

My Dear Friend,

Now that you've had a chance to reflect on the Prayer Notes that dealt with mysticism, I agree that it's a good time to return to that topic. In fact, I believe that "remysticalization" is one of the main tasks of today's pray-ers. Mysticism is particularly challenging in an age obsessed with "just the facts" and with surface spectacle. Mysticism goes beneath the surface to the awe and wonder at the heart of things. In our contemporary world it requires discovering the sacred significant in the insignificant and the divinely fantastic in the familiar.

In *Anam Cara* John O'Donohue writes, "Behind the facade of the familiar strange things await us. This is true of our homes, the place where we live, and, indeed, of those with whom we live. Friendships and relationships suffer immense numbing through the mechanism of familiarization. We reduce the wildness and mystery of person and landscape to the external, familiar image.... Familiarity enables us to tame, control, and ultimately forget the mystery."

What is forgotten is the mystery of the Divine Presence in yourself, in your world and at the heart of all creation. The great theologian Karl Rahner, who died in 1984, said there is really only one great Mystery with two aspects: the Mystery of a completely incomprehensible God and the Mystery of God's saving presence in the world. A mystic is simply that person who experiences, in a transforming manner, this saving Presence. This mystical experiencing does not have to include extraordinary phenomena; in fact, the sensational often obscures or overshadows our sense of the sacred. Moreover, today mystical potential is generally understood to belong to all persons and to be experienced right in the fabric of our daily lives.

You were born a latent mystic and a soul explorer. Developing this prenatal vocation is indispensable to your spirituality. Yet, if you believe that "mystichood" is only achieved by meticulously following exacting methods in ever-escalating stages, you will never leave home for Home!

Being your primal vocation, mystichood requires an everyday expedition to discover the Divine Mystery hidden incognito in the commonplace. Your soul is safari-ready, yet you are apt to dillydally dealing with daily demands. While exciting, this greatest of all quests can also be exhausting and frustrating. Nothing defies penetration like the familiar, as John O'Donohue says. The familiar tends to be immensely numbing and so can paralyze your soul's spirit of discovery.

Be hopeful, however, for the Invisible aches to become visible; the Holy Hidden craves to be revealed. Pray for the grace of a soul explorer willing and eager to struggle to break open and remystify your domesticated, mundane world. Your Hidden God immersed in all things is like a hide-and-seek child eager to be discovered and ready to gift you with desire. So passionately desire to seek out the source and remember the Mystery with all your heart and soul.

My Dear Friend,

Whether or not one is Catholic, the rosary can be a marvelous meditative prayer. While not as popular today as it was forty or fifty years ago, it has great potential, especially if you pray the original rosary. Today's practice is to pray each set of ten beads — each decade — after reflecting on a mystery, on one of the central events in the life of Mary or Jesus. The now-traditional rosary has five decades, each decade beginning with a mystery or life event of Jesus or Mary. These rosary mysteries are divided into three categories — Joyful, Sorrowful and Glorious — each containing five mysteries.

The prayer of the rosary appeared around the thirteenth century with the emergence of a special devotion to Mary, the Mother of Christ. Originally it required reflecting one by one on fifty different joyful experiences in the life of Mary and, after each of these mysteries, reciting the Hail Mary. A century later the sorrowful events, like the crucifixion, were added to these joyful reflections — and then even later the glorious experiences, such as the resurrection, were added. Because it was such a monumental task to memorize 150 different meditations, they were compiled in a book. However, this resolution did not help the vast majority of people, who at that time were illiterate, and so around the time of Columbus there was a reformation of the rosary. The changes made then reflect today's common form of only five meditations, one for each of the decades prayed.

If you wish to revisit and invigorate this prayer, I suggest you return to the original rosary of fifty different mysteries, praying a Hail Mary after each one. Non-Catholics, of course, could use the Lord's Prayer following the same pattern. I assure you that praying the old-fashioned rosary, visualizing fifty joyful mysteries in the life of Mary, will require the full use of your imagination.

Scripture is tight-lipped, relating only a small fraction of the daily events in the lives of Jesus and Mary. So to create fifty joyful, fifty sorrowful and fifty glorious life events will require that you explore your own life experiences as a basis for your meditation. The by-product of this life-reflective rosary will be a new consciousness of how the ordinary daily events of your personal life also contain great mysteries of grace.

My Dear Friend,

As you reflect on the relationship of your mind and your soul, realize that your mind is attracted to dogmas and definitions. It hankers for logical explanations, savors well-defined methods and routine prayers, and takes delight in the sameness of ritual. As different as night is from day, so your soul is the opposite of your mind. Your soul is enchanted by poetry, myth and lyrical words of prayer. It finds delight in strange symbols and mysterious signs rather than practical illustrations.

As for dogmas, the soul has only one, the three-word creed "God is love." These three words comprise the entire collection of the soul's holy books. They are its Bible, Torah, Koran, Dhammapada and Vedas. Day by day, hour by hour, event by event, if you live as fully as possible out of your soul's holy scriptures, its skinny creed, you will be engaged in ceaseless prayer. In the process you will connect more and more to your Source and give endless pleasure to your soul.

My Dear Friend,

Meal prayers are beautiful relics of that previous age when countless daily activities were considered to be sacred times. A table blessing might be defined as a preface-prayer ritual of dedication for a holy action about to begin. So I may surprise you by this suggestion: Don't pray before you eat!

Instead of that traditional prayer, consider this alternative table ritual: You can begin by saying, "Let us pray," pausing briefly in silence. Continue with a smile of anticipation, inviting all those at table to lift their forks and deliberately consume the first bite of their meal. In silent gratitude slowly savor the various aromas and flavors of the food and then exclaim, "Ah, blessed are you, O Lord, for these delicious gifts."

Unlike the traditional prayers recited before you eat, this AT (After Tasting) prayer is flavored and energized by your sensual delight in the food. AT Prayer is a whole body-and-soul expression of gratitude flowing out of the experience of God's bounty. Prayer before meals, while beautiful and traditional, might be compared to politely expressing gratitude upon receiving a wrapped present. AT prayer is the delicious delight and gratitude in actually enjoying the gift.

This AT prayer of gratitude has many other possibilities in your life. It can also be prayed after your first sip of a cocktail or glass of wine, after a concert or sporting event, or the start of any activity. The AT Prayer rule is: First comes the taste or experience of the gift; then a genuine rush of gratitude rises to your lips.

Say
Thank you
A
Hundred
Times
A
Day
And
You will
Discover
That you
Are
A Millionaire.

My Dear Friend,

Benedictine Brother David Steindl-Rast writes about the creative effect of surprise in the act of being grateful. He says that the living spiritual giants he has encountered in his life all have been profoundly grateful people. One of the ways to become a *mahatma,* to grow a large soul, is by becoming addicted to being grateful, especially when being surprised.

Any unexpected gift is really a double gift because it is received with more than usual gratitude. We live in a wonder world crammed with gifts, yet they are so common that we usually are blinded to them being gifts. After all these years you know me and my infatuation with the history and family trees of words. In Middle English the act of being surprised literally means "to be seized," as when someone suddenly reaches out and grabs you. What a perfect image for being surprised: to be caught up by something without any warning.

Being grateful for all things under all circumstances is perhaps the preeminent quality for you to become Godlike. This should be easy since you live in a state of perpetual giftedness as a beloved of the Great Gift-Giver. Yet it's all too easy to become desensitized by the glut of gifts we are given daily and to settle into "expectation," which is the great villain of surprise.

To sensitize your soul, scheme to surprise yourself by

playfully suspending your expectations. Be playfully surprised when your car starts with a simple turn of the key — and break into gratitude. Do likewise with your telephone and computer, with your legs and eyes — or with anything that works the way it is expected to operate.

Select a certain day and turn it into one long, preplanned surprise party as you suspend your usual anticipation of expected outcomes, not only from machines and equipment, but also from people! At the end of this all-day-long sacred surprise party, tally up the number of times you were grateful and delighted. I propose that such a day will lead you to throw frequent surprise parties as a routine in your life. If you do, I further propose that you will be dumbfounded and flabbergasted at the change in yourself and your outlook on life.

My Dear Friend,

I'm glad you enjoyed my suggestion about being a spy for God, especially since you've felt guilty about failing to speak publicly about your religious beliefs. I delight in your recent successes as a mystical mole. Now that you've had some positive experience as an undercover agent for the Empire of God, perhaps you're ready to advance to the role of a Bolshevik-like bomb-throwing revolutionary! This assignment is to be an underground agent in the world of the Anti-Kingdom, which is teeming with ferocious competition, uncontrolled greed and the shameless exploitation of the weak by the strong. This gloomy world of the Dark Empire must be sabotaged by deliberate deeds of subversion by secret reactionaries like yourself.

Bolsheviks used homemade bombs since stores didn't sell such destructive devices. While instructions for making bombs can now easily be found on the Internet or in survival manuals, you won't need them to create the kind of explosive you're to use. The nature of the bomb you'll employ is expressed in that word "explosive." Its usual meaning, "to burst with destructive force," is a relatively recent, 19th century connotation. Originally, "explode" was a theatrical expression meaning "to drive off stage with hisses and boos" — a marriage of *ex*, meaning "out," and *eplaudere*, meaning "clap" — the latter being the source of our word applaud. While good acts were met with thunderous applause, bad acts were exploded off the stage in a crowd-entertaining form of exorcism. As these explosions were occasions of great delight for the audience, joy is likewise the main ingredient of your homemade revolutionary bomb.

Indeed, the most efficient way to exorcize evil off the stage of life is with joyful humor. Joy and humor are the Molotov cocktails, the makeshift incendiary bombs of Blessed Bolsheviks, who toss these hand grenades of delight into the Evil Empire's drab work camps. As a holy terrorist, your mission is to set off such ticking, tickling time bombs in depressing meetings and when you are confronted with gloomy, authority-thumping bureaucrats. When those seated on their rickety thrones of power attempt to intimidate you, just explode a smile in their direction. The Enemy's henchmen/women hate smilers, who by such revolutionary acts silently rob them of power. Laughter is the best device to explode the solemn respect religion's authoritarians demand for themselves and their ideas.

In the process of building your homemade bombs, make your home into a test lab to create and test-explode your gloom-buster bombshells. I encourage you to become like those terrorist-rebels who become walking bombs and blow up themselves along with their targets. Begin at home whenever you find yourself acting pompous — explode your self-image right in front of your children and family. Before you leave home for work, always strap on your homemade bombs, which can be detonated whenever you find yourself being judgmental, self-important or pessimistic. Good disciple-spies for the Kingdom of Joy, be they at home or at work, in the world or in church, should always be kamikazes!

P.S. Be patient, as a spy of God, for the work of your sabotaging lightheartedness in service of the Great Revolution will not be achieved in your lifetime. However, when you grow weary of the struggle to overthrow the Enemy and are tempted to surrender to the Anti-Empire, constantly begin to repeat those radical words from your Sacred Spy Manual, "Rejoice always!"

My Dear Friend,

Columnist Jeannette Batz says that a home isn't a shell; rather, it's a process by which you are constantly discerning and reorganizing the stuff you need to live your life. She then asks the interesting question of whether we see our soul as a noun or a verb. I found this a fruitful reflection, since I am too often caught up in thinking of my soul as a sacred yet static noun-like reality.

As we can make our home more than a place of habitation, how might we make our soul an energetic, dynamic process, eternally in flux yet always at peace? Religious repetition causes us to think of the soul's activity as being situated in the next life — expressed in the prayer, "Eternal rest grant unto him, O Lord, and may his soul and all the souls of the faithful departed rest in peace."

Just as we can homestead, perhaps we can also soulstead. The old practice of homesteading begins with the hard work of cleaning the land for a home site. This ground clearing is followed by the construction of a dwelling, using materials close at hand. Then we humanize the house by inhabiting it as a home. Soulsteading begins in a similar way, with chopping down the dense grove of theological trees preventing organic soul development. Among these is the deeply rooted, centuries-old religious presentation of only two options for soul work: keeping our soul stain-free of sin and thus saving it, or losing it. Instead of showing ways to cultivate our souls, religion seems intent on making our souls static.

After clearing your inner space of whatever limits the building of your soul, next construct your soulstead by using whatever materials are at hand: your personality, your ethnic or family roots, your love relationships, your work and play. Your soulstead now completed, begin to live within it as your home. Let your soul soak up the aromas and pungent smells of your daily life, absorb your dreams and be saturated with the incense of your prayers and the sweat of your labors. Next, decorate your soulstead with beautiful music, art and extraordinary memories. By thus inhabiting your soul as your home, you and your soul will become intimately one.

Recall Jeannette Batz's suggestion that a home is not a thing, but is a process of constantly discerning and reorganizing the stuff you need to live your life. Your soulstead becomes larger and more beautiful when you daily invest it with prayer, compassionate deeds and expressions of love. Be aware that your soulstead needs frequent closet cleanings as you evaluate the needs of your inner life. This will require removing spiritual devotions, ideas and exercises that were once helpful in order to make room for newer, life-giving ones. This activity also requires evaluating the priorities of your soul life. Some old spiritual practices are now only holy antiques to be lovingly stored away in the attic of your soul, while what is now vital moves into the living room.

Letting fresh air circulate freely in your fully inhabited soul will keep you forever youthful and energetic. Your soulstead will be a mobile home, a heavenly habitat forever homeward bound.

P.S. A couple of prayer samples for cultivating an active soul life:

"May my soul be constantly fermenting, as restless as a horse in a burning barn, eager to grow into full maturity in Christ."

"In this world may I strive restlessly to live as soulfully as possible — until I finally relax in you, Divine Creator of my soul."

Notice how in the second part of this last prayer the request isn't that your soul stagnantly "rest in peace," but rather that "I," which includes your entire person — your body, soul, memories, personality and identity — will endlessly relax, vacationing in the abiding bliss of God.

Anyone
WITHOUT A
Soul friend
IS
LIKE
A
BODY
WITHOUT
A
HEAD.

ST. BRIDGET of IRELAND

My Dear Friend,

In our recent visit you told a story about an evening you spent with a good friend. I would encourage you to ponder on the relationship between prayer and friendship. For in love and friendship souls are woven together more tightly than hearts and minds. This weaving is done on God's loom with translucent soul threads light as an angel's breath but imperishable. Emotional bonds and communion in thought, being more tangible, are more easily experienced. A relationship of deep friendship and love, however, creates a communion at a profound level, at what could be called *soul-space.*

Sharing soul-space has the capacity to shrink spatial separations. Regardless of your geographic separation, it can allow you to be closer to a beloved in body and soul than when you are together in social space. Two persons separated by physical distance can come together by an inter-souling, the visiting of one soul with another. Your awareness of a soul-visitation by a friend or loved one can appear so subtle as to be almost imperceptible. To be more intellectually conscious of such a fleeting soul-visit, your mind must first acknowledge that such a reality can exist. Without this prelude belief, your mind will logically explain away or dismiss this mysterious but profound reality.

Whether or not the mind accepts this soul-ability as a rational reality, it does exist. Consider how common is, for example, the unexplainable phenomena of having a fleeting thought of someone just before receiving a telephone call or letter from that person. We usually say something like, "That's interesting, I was just thinking about you." Then the innocent intuition of a soul visit is quickly forgotten and rarely, if ever, pondered. Yet is it possible that this common phenomenon is an experience of sharing soul-space?

What is the source of such experiences of the soul? A deeply affectionate and focused love has the power to shrink physical distances between two persons, uniting them in body and soul. Particularly in a life-threatening crisis, our inner resources can be so aroused that even at great distances our loved ones become suddenly and thoroughly present. The deeper the union, as with mother and child, the more surely and more strongly does potential danger link us together.

Prayer is the superior space from which you can engage in transoulportation. By this means your soul can travel to the bedside of a sick loved one and attend funerals, weddings or other significant occasions at which you are unable to be physically present. This soul presence is more than mere thinking about the person and more than what usually takes place in the pious expression, "I'll pray for you that day." In fact, the awesome energies of the power of love and prayer cannot be comprehended or personally mobilized. The capacity of your soul to circumvent the barriers of space and time exists because of its eternal

Source and Sustainer — God. When your soul is deeply absorbed in prayer — in God — untold things are possible that your mind judges as impossible.

P.S. A couple of days after writing this reflection I was reading Paul's Letter to the Colossians. This letter was written to a small Christian community in faraway Asia Minor while Paul was a prisoner, perhaps in Rome. At the beginning of the second chapter he writes, "For even if I am absent in the flesh, yet I am with you in spirit." I'm certain that Paul was truly *with* his friends in Colossae.

My Dear Friend,

I write to you about the Prayer of Consouling. That's not a misspelling; rather, it's a new word for the sacred action of the commingling of souls. This prayer can be used before going to console a friend or neighbor suffering the loss of a loved one, or on your way to attend a wake or funeral. Authentic consolation is participation in the exodus sacrament of consoulation. In this sacrament you first exit out of your self so you can become one with those who are grieving. Both genuine consoling and true congratulating are out-of-body experiences. These twin gestures are usually simply expressions of good manners that require adopting a certain tone of voice with the appropriate facial features of either sadness or happiness. Consouling isn't the same as sympathy, which often might only be feeling sorry for another's suffering and not actually sharing in the person's pain.

Genuine consolation is Godly, the holy communion of souls. In a previous note we reflected on how by prayer you have the power to give wings to your soul in order to travel to the aid of another. Recall also how soul power flowed spontaneously out of Jesus and healed a woman of her long-suffering disease after she had simply touched the hem of his robe. Follow her example of faith and with deep trust in Christ ask to be "healed" of the perceived division separating you from the other who is suffering.

To be able to console another requires first being healed of the self-absorption that cripples your capacity to be other-absorbed. This universal affliction is more a consequence of our human evolution than the result of primordial sin. Still loitering deep in our subterranean flesh are evolutionary, pre-human tendencies rooted in the need for survival. Whenever we encounter terrible suffering or death in someone we do not love, an ancient unhealed part of us is secretly grateful that we were not the victim of that evil misfortune.

Because of this primeval disposition, the ability to be authentically compassionate with others in their sorrow or their joy requires an exodus, a departure out of your self-concerned self. This is an evolutionary act of rising upward to enter your Christ-self. While your primal self-serving self aches to act first in any situation, by practice, prayer and grace, your Christ-self can override the immature self, and you can reach out to others in need.

Whenever you are called upon to respond with consolation to someone who is grieving, quickly pray for the grace to receive the sacrament of consouling. Trust that God will swiftly answer your prayer. Rising above your natural fear of pain, allow the Holy Soothing Spirit to unite your soul with the one drowning in grief. Spoken words are inadequate in expressing sympathy, and so we often feel impotent in the face of grief. By the act of consoling, however, we're freed of having to say anything significant since whatever we say will be saturated with the presence of our soul, which truly has the power to console those who mourn.

P.S. In Jesus' beatitude "Blessed are they who mourn, for they will be consoled" is hidden another beatitude, "Blessed are they who comfort those who mourn, for they shall be greatly consoled by God." This is a building blessing: The Acts of the Apostles tells how the infant apostolic church grew in numbers *"by means of the consolation of the Holy Spirit."*

Consolation is a type of construction. Whenever you comfort another, Spirit power builds you up in the fullness of Christ. So rejoice in every opportunity to exodus from sympathy into consolation, since by so doing you are growing in Christhood. The divine comedy of contradictions says that by exiting out of yourself you actually are entering into your true self.

My Dear Friend,

In response to your recent letter, I would like to propose that you consider praying the Litany *for* the Saints, which is different from the Litany *of* the Saints. Let's begin with the term *saints*, which today is commonly reserved for those who are now united in eternity with God. Early Christians, however, addressed each other as saints, as *the holy ones*, and perhaps if we returned to that practice we might be awakened to striving to become in this life what we wish to be in the one that follows.

The Litany for the Saints is a prayer of intercession. The names of the saints are those of living family and friends and those in need: a pregnant daughter-in-law, a nephew in need of work, a dear friend undergoing surgery or a neighbor bearing the painful loss of a lifelong spouse. The Litany for the Saints touches directly upon the mystery of intercessory prayer, which, in turn, is at the heart of transformative prayer. John Newman said the fallen person prays for him/herself, while the redeemed person prays for others.

I would like to suggest a practice I myself began some time ago with my intercessory prayers. I created my own litany of names of those for whom I daily petition God, typing out a list and putting it in a small cardboard folder that I keep at my prayer shrine. My personal Litany for the Saints includes my family and old friends who by their love have so generously gifted me in life and the names of those with whom I share the soul-journey (by the way, your name is included among the saints in this litany). Besides these names permanently inscribed in my prayer litany, I also pencil in the prayer requests of those who have asked me, "Would you please pray for...?" We are blessed with that beautiful religious tradition of asking others to join us in praying for special needs.

Whenever someone asks me to remember some need or person in my prayers, I take seriously my prayer pledge and immediately jot down the intention. When I return home, I pencil in the petition in my permanent Litany for the Saints. Daily I pray for the intention until I hear that the special need no longer exists. My practice is to remember the intention for at least forty days before erasing it from my unchanging litany. While I usually neglect to make this verbal response, I think a good practice when asked to be a prayer-person for another would be to say, "I will be honored to join you in praying for that intention."

This Litany for the Saints has a Scriptural foundation. Saint Paul implored us to look upon the needs of the saints as our own. We do this both by caring for their material needs and by remembering them in our prayers. The needs of your neighbors who live across the street and your neighbors who live across the world can also have a place in your litany of petitions. As the Master taught us, praying for your enemies also belongs in your litany. It is especially important to include those whom you find difficult to forgive.

Intercessory prayer shares in the Mystical Communion of the Saints, for anyone you remember in prayer is made present in your heart and soul. Praying for the needs of others with the same zeal you would give to your own needs impresses upon you the reality of how you and they are bound together in the Body of Christ. As a result of remembering others' intentions in your prayer, your consciousness and the radius of your soul are expanded.

P.S. I thank you for your kindness in calling to tell me the good results of your medical test. Whenever someone asks for a prayer gift, it is spiritually gracious to inform the pray-er about the outcome of the request.

P.P.S. One last thought. Just before sending this note off to you, I was visiting on the phone with a friend who is a religious sister. She said that when she is asked to pray for someone's "special intention," she is able to pray with more fervor if she knows the actual need of the person. I agreed with her — it's a great prayer aid even when the need seems unspeakable.

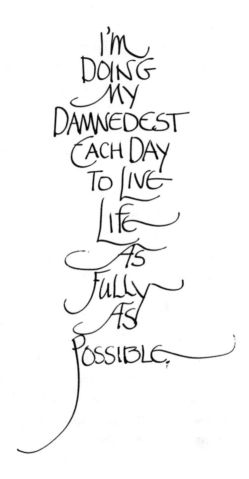

I'M DOING MY DAMNEDEST EACH DAY TO LIVE LIFE AS FULLY AS POSSIBLE,

My Dear Friend,

As a soul companion, you are well aware that one of my favorite quotations is from Meister Eckhart, who said that the way to holiness is simply to do the next thing you have to do with all your heart and soul, and with delight. I keep a copy of that quote on my desk to remind me how I might achieve my primal vocation of becoming Godlike.

As I was reflecting this morning, I came to a new insight regarding prayer. Previously in my Prayer Notes I've spoken about trying to invest my prayers with as much love as possible. It occurred to me that I also need to love *my prayers* with all my heart and soul! I realized that if I am to love God well, I must romance my praying with great affection and delight.

When we love what we are doing, that task is accomplished not only with great joy but also with originality. Those who love to cook create delicious meals with even the simplest of ingredients, and it's the same when you love to pray. When you delight in praying, your prayers will naturally become creative and beautiful. A hidden aspect of loving whatever you do is that in the process your ego-self is kidnapped. Like authors, artists and athletes who love what they do, musicians report that a marvelous thing happens when they forget themselves and are totally lost playing their music. Rather than them playing the music, the music mysteriously seems to play through them. When accomplished singers are passionate about their art, the songs seem to sing themselves.

So, in your desire to be an artist of prayer, forget about trying to create original new prayers. Simply fall in love with praying! Then any of your prayers will be stunningly beautiful. This short note about the big task of passionately loving your praying á la Meister Eckhart holds the magic of transforming even your most insignificant prayer into a masterpiece.

My Dear Friend,

In our last conversation you spoke of your difficulty in accepting the dogma of the virginity of the mother of Jesus. In response, consider the thoughts of the delightful American author Flannery O'Connor, who provides an enchanting window into contemplative prayer. Writing to a friend, she said, "Dogma can in no way limit a limitless God. The person outside the church attaches a different meaning to it than a person in. For me a dogma is only a gateway to contemplation and is an instrument of freedom and not of restriction. It preserves mystery for the human mind."

Even though some Christians are willing to go to war over them, the dry dogmas of our faith usually have little impact on our daily lives. Most dogmas were declared in early historical ages of the church and so naturally bear the influence of the theology, politics, social attitudes and science of those long-past ages. Every Sunday, Christians stand to pray the Creed in which are proclaimed the most important of the dogmas of our faith. Perhaps I should say we "recite" rather than "pray" the Creed. While saying the simpler, more direct Apostles Creed could be a prayerful expression, the Nicene Creed has such complicated philosophical twists and theological turns that it seems less a prayer than an oral examination for heretics.

I like Flannery O'Connor's idea that dogmas are only gateways to contemplation. For your reflection, consider taking only one statement of belief out of the Creed and using it as a doorway to contemplate what personal treasures of soul-growth it may contain for you. If you choose "...he was born of the Virgin Mary and became man," instead of a knee-jerk gesture of belief, play with your disbelief. Since in the natural order it is impossible for a virgin to become pregnant and give birth, reflect on something desirable in your life that seems impossible. Then prayerfully recall how when Mary expressed her disbelief in the possibility of a virginal birth, the angel told her, "Yes, but with God all things are possible."

Or take the opening sentence of the Nicene Creed. If it was truly prayed instead of just robotically recited, the result could be stunning. When saying those nine words, "We believe in one God, the Father, the Almighty," it is awful that we are habitually so aweless. If we stood and prayed to that All Powerful, All Supreme, All Knowing and Unknowable, All Inclusive of all that exists and All Present God, how could we remain standing? This first of all dogmas should open the floodgates to awe and trembling whenever we come into the presence of the God of Hosts for prayer and worship. What is remarkable is the absence of believers' reverent awe when they enter a sacred place where their belief states that God dwells. Should we not shudder in holy fear when the Divine Presence is called down to witness vows and blessings or when we are handling sacred objects we believe to be radioactive with the holy? More often than not, what we actually proclaim is our casual chumminess at worship and prayer.

Who is to blame? The accusing finger has been pointed at our casual, dress-down, convenience-first culture. Some claim it is the confusion that arose when we shifted to a horizontal, communal worship from a vertical, divine worship. Paradoxically, the popular slang term "awesome" now applies to everything even marginally stunning and breathtaking, yet it is never used about worship or prayer. Perhaps if we follow the finger of blame back far enough, it will finally end up at the nose of Jesus of Nazareth! Didn't the Master teach us to approach God as a beloved, loving parent, as "Abba," rather than with trembling and fear? In the Exodus desert days of the Hebrew people, if anyone even accidentally touched the golden Ark of the Convent, it meant instant death. By contrast, Jesus the Prophet taught that God wanted to be touched, especially to be lovingly handled when we care for the suffering, outcasts and the poor.

Which, then, is the correct stance for us: fear and trembling, or closeness and intimacy? Or is it perhaps both? While we presently have a familiar, informal intimacy, should we not somehow regain a sense of reverential awe at the Divine Mystery? And should we not integrate that awe into our desire for intimate relationship? Perhaps the way to achieve this is to begin to ponder the seeming contradictions in our dogmatic beliefs — such as the Virgin Birth and the Divine Humanity. For as Flannery O'Connor wrote, this process "...preserves mystery for the human mind."

My Dear Friend,

This note is a follow-up to my previous note about awe and holy fear. Being caught up in holy dread and wonder needs to be expanded beyond times of worship and sacred places. As the inspired writer of the First Letter of Peter wrote, "In prayer you call upon a Father who judges each one justly, on the basis of his/her actions. Since this is so, *conduct yourselves reverently during your sojourn in a strange land.*"

Scripture scholar John Pilch points out that in this text the word *reverently* literally means "with fear or reverent awe." Jesus said that the world would recognize his disciples by how they love one another. Another sign of being a child of God, who is immersed in every facet of our lives, is the capacity to go about life with a sense of holy astonishment. Sojourning from event to event overwhelmed with reverence for the humdrum is only possible if we think the world is waterlogged with the Wonderful, saturated with the Sacred. To be awestruck by the ordinary has to be the greatest challenge of all mystics-to-be.

Twenty-first century mystics will be identified not because they are always in church praying, but because they constantly shudder in awe and are staggered by wonder: Absorbed in adoration, they stagger on their sojourn from sacred place to sacred place. They will be known as holy not because they keep pious practices but because they are daily dazzled by the Divine, not because of penitential self-flagellation but because they are wholly flabbergasted with God.

P.S. The Holy Spirit speaks the same message from another tradition. In the Upanishads, the scriptures of India, it says, "Unless it is wonderful, wonderful, it cannot be holy."

My Dear Friend,

Transcendental Meditation became popular in the late 1960s after the famous rock group the Beatles adopted it. For many it continues to be the preferred method for meditation. Now when I'm asked what form of meditation I practice, my answer is, "These days I find myself increasingly becoming an Unpremeditator."

By its very nature institutional religion is cemented to preplanned, structured methods, rituals and disciplines. To be sure, in any art methods and discipline are necessary and can be fruitful. Daily agendas of physical and spiritual exercises ensure the formation of good habits, which, in turn, bear positive results. However, we might ask if it is possible for a spiritual seeker to graduate from structured methods and rituals. That's not to say graduation would be easy. Aged, automatic, disciplined devotions tend toward the robotic. For that reason, and especially because they are so comforting, they aren't easily dropped. Moreover, religion reinforces non-spontaneity by requiring that prayer be in the form of precisely performed rituals of changeless repetition.

For unpremeditators, on the other hand, prayer and contemplation often erupt spontaneously for no apparent cause. It's a rare and precious gift, but it shouldn't be that uncommon because, like mysticism, it's available to all of us. Yet unpremeditators are so unusual because spontaneity is scarce in our highly organized daily life and spirituality.

Religion is highly suspicious of spontaneity, and public worship generally forbids extemporaneous prayer and ritual. Ah, another paradox — for your undomesticated soul delights in unrehearsed, effortless expressions of love and devotion.

Of course, the counterpoint is that the soul's ability to engage in spontaneous prayer usually requires years of structured spiritual discipline. As with any art form, the classical approach first involves learning the principles and structures before attempting to engage in wildly improvised prayer. However, anyone can profitably incorporate times of spontaneous prayer into his or her disciplined practice.

Besides, you, my friend, are no longer a novice at prayer and spirituality. Could now be the time for you to become an unpremeditator? Trust in God's love for you and your love of God, and trust that from this ground of love your soul will respond spontaneously to your Beloved. Spontaneity is a dear friend of the soul, even as it is the archenemy of the ego, which constantly is on guard not to be out of control. Your ego, in fact, dreads any spontaneous joyful combustion of your soul bursting into fiery life.

Being liberated enough to become unpremeditated can begin with romancing frequent acts of spontaneity. Taste soulful excitement in seized opportunities to be extemporaneous in your behavior; ad-lib your love for God and others. Buy surprise gifts for non-occasions; celebrate impromptu holidays; go off on unplanned mini-adventures; and learn to live, love and pray with soulful unpremeditation.

My Dear Friend,

Nothing invokes guilt like the question, "How's your prayer life?" Few, if any, of us feel we know how to properly pray or that we pray enough. This abiding sense of personal failure can easily cause us to abandon praying altogether, except in times of crisis. Among my favorite parables is a story by Rabbi Israel Friedman about a small Jewish village far off the main path:

> Once upon a time there was a small Jewish village that had all the necessary facilities, a law court, a hospital and a cemetery; as well as the usual assortment of craftsmen — shoemakers, tailors, bakers and carpenters. The village, however, lacked one trade: a watchmaker. Over many years the clocks in the town became so annoyingly inaccurate that many of their owners stopped winding them anymore and just ignored them.

> However, there were a few people in the village who believed that as long as their clocks were running they should not be discarded. Day after day they religiously wound their clocks, even though they no longer kept the correct time. Their neighbors made fun of them: "How silly to keep winding your clock when it doesn't keep accurate time." But one day the good news

traveled like lightning that a master watchmaker
had just moved into the village. Everyone rushed
to his house with their clocks. To their dismay,
they discovered the only ones he could repair were
those that had been kept running, for the
abandoned clocks had grown too rusty to fix.

The only bad prayer is no prayer. Even prayers that
may be rushed, theologically inaccurate and tinged with
superstition are still significant expressions of devotion.
Regardless of how poverty-ridden your prayers may seem, do
not delegate the practice of praying to supposed experts like
contemplative monks and nuns. And while it is always good
to learn more about prayer, improve it and deepen it, be
careful to refrain from judging your prayers. When you're in
the midst of praying, do not evaluate the quality or value of
your prayers; just pray them. As in the parable of the clocks,
simply be faithful to daily winding your prayer-clock.

A wholesome daily diet of prayer has a combination of
regularity and spontaneity. Scheduling times of prayer in
the morning, the evening and at the dinner hour, regardless
of how brief, creates a rhythm as well as a regularity in your
prayer life. It also invites the energy force of the Spirit into
your inspired spontaneous expressions of gratitude, petition
and wonder. Disciplined daily times of prayer and spur-of-
the-moment occasions are the Siamese twins of prayer. They
mutually reinforce and nourish each other.

These two prayer partners often exchange gifts: Certain phrases from daily formal prayers may suddenly appear in your spontaneous prayer, and fresh spur-of-the-moment praise may at times enliven your prescribed prayers. These prayer twins are powerful agents working together to create a good soul environment for growth in the capacity to pray ceaselessly, which is the goal of a fruitful spiritual life.

P.S. As in Rabbi Friedman's parable, fortunate are those who continue to pray daily, even when they feel their prayers are sadly inadequate. For they can call upon the Spirit, the master Prayermaker, to adjust their prayers as necessary. As Paul of Tarsus said, none of us really knows how to pray, but the Spirit takes our groaning and moaning efforts and transforms them into stunningly beautiful love songs so precious to the heart of God.

My Dear Friend,

Thanks for picking up the tab from our lunch the other day. I would like to echo my encouragement that you become the Fred Astaire of shadow dancers. You told me with typical Irish enthusiasm that you were declaring war on your demons and wanted to engage in some do-it-yourself exorcism. I suggested a reflection on the story of Jesus in the desert after his baptism, where Mark says that he was with the wild beasts, and then angels came to minister to him. You were surprised when I raised the question: What if those angels were previously the wild beasts whom he had tamed? I then encouraged you, instead of shadow boxing with your demons, to try shadow dancing with them.

While spiritual guides down through the centuries have promoted an athletic asceticism and encouraged a spiritual warfare against inner darkness, such an approach is frequently counterproductive. Conversion rather than destruction is the path of Gospel transformation, and the most effective weapon in this campaign is love. I agree with the American writer Henry Miller, who said, "The full and joyful acceptance of the worst in oneself may be the only sure way of transforming it." Those are powerful words; they suggest how self-defeating it is to hate those dark aspects of ourselves of which we are ashamed. Even more destructive are attempts to perform exorcisms on our inner beasts, seeking to drive them away instead of converting them into our personal angels who might then assist us.

Henry Miller calls for the full and joyful acceptance of that which is the worst in us. Fully accepting your shadows requires seeing all of who you are — even those parts that are wounded and disowned — as good and beautiful. This wholesome vision of yourself is critical for the essential soul-work of your transformation into a living image of the Divine Mystery. Remember that conversion, not rejection, is God's way. When you convert a dark, dank basement into a warm family room, you don't destroy that space; you renovate it into something useful. Do the same with the dark recesses of your soul and the shadows that reside there. Often what is viewed as a dark failing is only some good trait that has become distorted, bent out of shape by selfishness.

While everything is good, not everything is good for you all the time. Some tendencies and behaviors may not be appropriate for you at this juncture of your spiritual journey, and your transformation may require abstaining from them. It may be premature to experience some things, and what once was good and enjoyable may later in life become destructive and addictive. Some aspects of your self may become so twisted that moving with them will only take you down a dead-end road. Remember, though, however dark and sinister your shadows may be, never judge them as evil. Rather, take them in hand and patiently do a dance of transformation.

Along with a *full* acceptance, the second half of Henry Miller's equation is the more difficult task in transforming the worst in oneself: a *joyful* acceptance. Whatever is judged to be shameful is usually denied or disguised. Societies and institutions as well as individuals expend great amounts of energy attempting to camouflage whatever they consider evil and foul within them. This denial of darkness spawns a perpetual state of an anxious fear of disclosure. The greatest of all commandments, love of God and neighbor, begins with the love of oneself — all of oneself.

Joy is the flower of love. To begin loving your shadows, look on the inside of their external darkness and try to see their potential good and beauty and rejoice in their hidden, as-yet-unexplored gifts. Having joyfully accepted your demons and shadows, invite them to become your friends, aware that your darkest demons can become your brightest, most helpful angels. If at times this dance seems too difficult, remember that the Master Dancer is always dancing with you and your shadows. When you keep this in mind, I assure you that you will find it easier to perform one of Jesus' most difficult commands, "Do not judge, do not condemn."

Pray for that Galilean gift of not throwing stones at others — or yourself. Pray, too, that if you're caught off guard by a surprise visit from one of your untamed shadows you can respond, "May I have this dance?"

My Dear Friend,

As you deal with having to make difficult decisions, realize that "I've changed my mind" is a declaration of repentance, which Jesus said is essential to entering the Kingdom of God.

While this expression is commonly used for changing from one choice to another, it can also mean exchanging your present state of mind for a different one. Paul spoke of the necessity of changing your mind when he wrote, "Put on the mind of Christ." The result of this mind exchange is that you would begin to think like, fantasize like, dream like and judge like Christ did with his mind.

Yet as you well know, your mind "has a mind of its own" and doesn't cherish being evicted. So even as you "change your mind," your old mind will continuously attempt to return to its former domicile. By daily prayerful reflection on your thoughts, your judgments and even your dreams, you will come to know whose mind you have in mind. Indeed, putting on the mind of Christ isn't as effortless as putting on a cap. This exchange is only achieved gradually, one thought at a time, replacing one judgment with another as you graduate to a new way of thinking. When an associate comments on one of your new attitudes, "That's just the opposite of what you used to say," you can reply, "Yes, I've changed my mind."

A core goal of the spiritual life is to be transformed. As

Paul said, "Do not conform yourself to this age but be transformed by the renewal of your mind." One infallible sign that you are being transformed is that you are constantly contradicting yourself — your old self.

The Kingdom, the Empire of God, in which you are called to dwell is itself an elusive state of being that defies any particular geographic location. This reflection concludes with a sentence by Winston Churchill that is worthy of meditation: "All the great empires of the future will be empires of the mind."

My Dear Friend,

As you further reflect on how you might "pray always," I'd like to suggest another practice: Ebony Prayer, or praying in bed. Not only can you pray ceaselessly but in all places as well, including the darkness of your sleep. Indeed, while your body is at rest, your soul spends the night in vigil, as at a wake. The prayers recited at the wake of a deceased person are mirrored nightly as your soul keeps prayerful vigil while you sleep.

When your constantly active mind is parked in the sleep mode, the deluge of billions of bits of information from your body sensors is turned off. This sleeptime stoppage of sensory information creates an unobstructed, creative space for your soul, your inner self, to assist your conscious self. As you rise to the surface from slumber, listen for the voice of your soul, which can deliver to you intuitive messages, new insights into difficult issues and solutions to the problems of your waking state.

The Chinese have a wise old adage that says: "Place your problem under your pillow and sleep on it." A contemporary variation of this ancient truth could be: "Even the poorest peasant has a personal sage whose name is Sleep. Consult this wisdom figure whenever you are in need of sage advice." Today's "I-want-it-now—at-this-instant" age makes it more difficult to delay making decisions and to sleep on the problems you face. Resist the temptation to be a Johnny- or Janey-on-the-spot, and give your soul a chance to pray over the issues, even for several nights if necessary. Be prayerfully patient. The resolution may come when you are awakened in the middle of the night or in those fertile twilight times of being half-awake.

It's easy to forget God's eagerness to come to our aid as beloved sons or daughters. Yours is only the responsibility of creating uncluttered soul-listening space. This space can be found by retreating to a solitary place — as we see in Jesus' frequent getaways during his times of crisis. It is also readily available when your sun-time prayer is wedded to your ebony-time prayer.

One simple Ebony Prayer ritual would be to pause before you get into bed and lift up your pillow; then symbolically place your problem on the sheet beneath it. Lovingly pat that resting place of your problem with a brief prayer-plea that God will chat with your soul as you sleep.

My Dear Friend,

This note begins with a parable called "The Man Who Tried to Hide from Death." There was a man who not only feared to die, but he didn't even want to think about his death. Living in this state of denial wasn't easy since he had the premonition he was constantly being pursued by death. It seemed to follow him everywhere, even into his bathroom mirror. So he tried to use disguises. He attempted to hide behind titles and honors and to conceal himself in his work. He tried to hide in sex and success. He tried to hide in the gym and in church.

Yet no matter where he tried to hide, it seemed that death was lurking nearby. Finally, frustrated, he shouted, "Where are you?"

As he fearfully looked all around, a velvety voice whispered, "Here! I'm here inside you."

Both holy twins, life and death, reside within you. Limitless life is the shape of your soul, eternally immune to death, decay and destruction. Death is the perpetual condition of your body from the moment of birth; death is constantly at work eroding away, inch by inch, your flesh and bone. Both of these holy twins have voices, if you have ears willing to listen.

Your death speaks to you about the urgency of growing your soul larger and larger by acts of love. Your death constantly admonishes you not to take for granted those you love and not to miss your countless opportunities to use productively your limited life span. Listen to your death.

Your soul's voice also constantly shares in this inner dialog, saying, "Do not be anxious, for that which you call final death is only a transformation of matter, since energy cannot be destroyed. The earthy substance of your flesh is transformed into another, more glorious and sacred substance. Your death within is only a door that leads to home; do not fear the hour it will open. Live watchful of that Grand Opening; be prepared."

The answer to how to prepare for death is with prayer. As you listen to the constant dialogue of the soul and death within you, daily pray for a good death. Not simply when attending a funeral or visiting a cemetery, keep that intention in your daily consciousness since it fine-tunes your ears to hear the guiding twin voices of your soul and your death. Praying for a happy death becomes a living blueprint for the Grand Opening and the golden years that preface it.

> O Loving God,
> grant me a rich harvest of retirement years,
> and a happy and peaceful death.

As you pray this prayer every day, remember what the Master promised: "Ask and you shall receive."

My Dear Friend,

As you continue to reflect on death, here is a dialog fit for meditation:

God, at the moment of your death, says, "Come, my beloved, it's time for us to go."

Naturally, you ask, "Go where?"

"Nowhere."

"But, God, didn't you just say it was time to go?"

"Yes, it's time to go — to be transformed into the present so that you can be here and now, as I am."

When you pray for your beloved dead, where do you think they are? Are they in some far distant place called heaven, or are they right here beside you in a parallel universe, thinly veiled from the one in which you presently live?

EVERY
DEATH
LEAVES
A
CALLING
CARD

Sorry I missed you. I'll be back your way — soon.
Death

My Dear Friend,

Healthy are those who live daily with the mystery of death, their own and that of loved ones. Such a daily consciousness should include the prayer of Good Grief. Moreover, this prayer should be practiced well in advance of the time of grieving so that you will be prepared when Death's Dark Angel visits your life.

You've increasingly come to appreciate how loving another does not require the actual presence of the beloved, and that physical separation does not sever the bonds of affection. Those who love one another experience a sense of loss whenever they are apart, even if only for a day. This sadness is a form of lovers' sorrow that could be called Good Grief because it actually strengthens the bonds of love. The next time you and your loved ones part company — whether to go off to work or school or shopping — and you experience being physically separated from them for hours, pray the prayer of Good Grief. As you experience their departure, also experience your unity with them in that special holy communion that knows neither distance nor separation.

Whenever you think about them or pray for them, you can visualize them at the place where they are likely to be at that time of day. As you do this, be lovingly conscious of the bonds that unite you as one. Frequent acts of long-distance communion permeate your relationship with grace and love. And doing so with the prayer of Good Grief makes these moments preparations for the ultimate departure and separation of death.

When Good Grief becomes a reality in daily life, it will be so much more profound at the time of death, even if death's separation lasts for more than a few hours or a few days. Whatever the anguish of death you experience, it can be Good Grief when it is married to the reality of communion. Although in the separation of daily life you can envision the surroundings of your beloved, sadly in death this is not possible. The faces of your loved ones are the windows of their souls and are, in turn, indelibly imprinted upon your soul. Allow their faces, which by death are now perpetually youthful, to become a holy threshold over which you can cross, in Good Grief, to be united with them — wherever they are. Different societies have varying periods of time considered proper to grieve over the dead. Good Grief is different. While it enables you to go on with your life and live fully, it is also a lifelong sacrament of bereavement of oneness until you finally join your beloved deceased in the ecstasy of eternal love.

My Dear Friend,

The Native Americans held that the stars were created by the ascending souls of the dead. They believed that those stars pierced holes in the sky curtain, allowing the Light to shine through. As a luminous memorial to one you deeply loved, go outside at night on a star-clustered night and select a particularly bright star. Rename it after your deceased beloved, and then also give new names to several more stars in honor of others you loved whose souls have pierced the heavens.

A good celestial meditation would be to reflect on how the light you see from a faraway star may have left that star 10,000 or even 10,000,000 light-years ago. In fact, the star-source of that beautiful light might now no longer exist. Let the Eternal Light of your holy dead shine upon you both night and day, just as all the stars do. In the daytime we are blinded to their presence by the brilliance of our closest star, the sun. The same, I might propose, is true for our deceased, whose presence is obscured by the glare and noise of our work-a-day life.

Celestial meditation isn't easy, for we have been housebroken and rarely go outdoors to spend time in the dark under the stars. Even if we did, we are also citified, and so their brilliance is muted if not eclipsed by the glare of millions of electric lights. As an alternative to the church's great night prayer of compline, you might drive out into the countryside beyond the brightly lit dome of the city. Stop your car, get out, behold the night sky and be swept away by the glory of the Milky Way of Saints. In silence prayerfully locate your special holy star or stars and enter into communion with your luminous deceased, allowing their starlight to saturate your soul.

I can think of nothing more beautiful that could be said about you or me at our death than the words Shakespeare used in his play *Romeo and Juliet*:

> ...and, when he shall die,
> Take him and cut him out in little stars,
> And he will make the face of the heaven so fine
> That all the world will be in love with night.

Author's Acknowledgments

This book would not have been possible without the help of those good friends with whom I have shared the great privilege of being a soul-friend. The raw material for this book flows from our conversations about prayer, spirituality and the struggle to live out authentically the wise sayings of Jesus. I thank them for their insights and also for trusting me as their soul-friend.

I wish this book's cover was at least three times larger so there would be room for the names of all who shared in its creation. I wish to express my gratitude and to say that along with the author's name, the following names rightfully belong on the front of this book:

Thomas Skorupa, my dedicated and tireless editor. With great love and attention he has sandpapered smooth and grammatically corrected my manuscript. I am fortunate among authors, for it is a rare gift to have a friend who has been editor of all but one of the twenty-six books that carry my name.

Thomas Turkle's name also belongs on the cover because he has invested so much time and thought in the publishing of this book. He is my friend and harshest critic, my arch-encourager and idealistic balloon burster, the book's designer, production coordinator and publisher.

The names of Steve Hall and the employees of Hall Commercial Printing of Topeka also deserve a place on the cover. I have known Steve for forty years, and he has been the printer for Forest of Peace Publishing since my first book. I thank him for his flexibility and his dedication to the art of printing. The craftsmen and artisans at Hall Commercial Printing, by their friendliness and enthusiasm, have transformed the work of manufacturing a book into a celebration of life.

My unnamed proofreaders also deserve a place on the cover because their tireless third eyes have searched as best as humanly possible for missing commas, stray question marks and other grammatical errors that may have evaded my editor.

Finally, the cover should bear the names of each of you reading this book, for it wouldn't have been written and published without you!

The Author

At the date of the publication of this book, the author Edward Hays had surpassed by two years the famed ripe age described in Psalm 90, "Threescore and ten is the sum of our years, fourscore if we are strong, most of them are sorrow...." He hopes to reach fourscore, or eighty, and that, strengthened by the Spirit, these will not be years of sorrow but of creativity and joyful zest. Invigorated by the Ever-young Spirit, he even hopes he may reach the sum of fourscore and ten and do so abounding in joy! While today many wring their hands bemoaning this gloomy age of the world and religion, the author considers these times as only the turbulent labor pains that come with pregnancy. When asked why he wished to live such a long life, he smiled and replied, "I am enthusiastically eager for the arrival of these years of enormous growth and transformation of society and religion. The next twenty years will bring radical religious and social changes together with amazing advances in technology, communication, science, medicine and the arts. My desire to reach fourscore and ten years is more than simply to be alive and witness these radical changes; I passionately desire to be their cheerleader and midwife."

His college education and post-graduate studies were at the hands of the innovative Benedictine monks of Conception Abbey in Conception, Missouri. They prophetically prepared him for the future radical changes in the church of the Second Vatican Council while immersing him in their ancient spirit of prayer and spirituality. He confesses without shame that he never actually graduated from college! To prove this, he pointed to a small bronze plaque paperweight on his desk on which were inscribed the words, "*I am still learning.* —Michelangelo."

Ordained a priest in 1958, four years later he claims he was re-ordained by the Spirit as a disciple, servant of the people and torchbearer of the vision of Vatican II. After twelve years as a parish priest, he spent the next twenty-three years as the director of Shantivanam, a lay community of contemplative prayer. His last, and what he calls his "golden," years of ministry were spent as a prison chaplain at the Kansas State Penitentiary. He retired from the active ministry in 2001, and continues writing and dabbling in the arts, along with continuing his previous work as a spiritual consultant and soul companion for others.